Who Should Read This Book

This book is not just for Jewish people. It is for all people who would gain strength to heal and insight from Jewish tradition.

- ✓ Anyone who is seeking an understanding of the Twelve Steps from a Jewish perspective —regardless of religious background or affiliation

- ✓ Alcoholics and Addicts in Recovery and all people who are in trouble with alcohol and drugs and other addictions—food, gambling, and sex

  - Affiliated Jews: Reform, Conservative, Reconstructionist, Orthodox

  - All other Jews who seek guidance from a shared and sacred tradition

  - People of all faiths who seek both guidance and renewal through recovery

- ✓ Codependents

  - Anyone who is in an addictive relationship

- Anyone who was raised in a dysfunctional family
- Adult Children of Alcoholics
✓ Specialists in Recovery
  - Friends who care
  - Rabbis, priests and ministers, spiritual counselors of all kinds
  - Alcohol and chemical dependency counselors
  - Psychiatrists, psychologists, therapists

The first step says it all; it establishes a foundation for everything else. Alcohol (or drugs, eating, sex, or gambling) is making a mess of your life because you are addicted or care deeply about someone who is. Even if you are not addicted or do not know someone who is, this book will offer you the inspiration to face the challenges of life and daily living. In one broad admission, the first step epitomizes the entire Twelve Step program. This process of recovery has proven itself effective for thousands of people—providing they worked the program. Each step is worked through over and over again, moving us forward in recovery every time we move through the steps, whether simultaneously or one at a time.

As Jews we are taught that God spoke at Mount Sinai in 600,000 voices—one for each Israelite who had fled Egyptian slavery, surrounding Sinai, waiting for God's revelation. 600,000 voices, so that each individual could understand in his or her own way.

Such is the case with this guide. Many Jewish voices are heard in each step. Religious voices, humanist voices, and just plain people's voices. Search out your own. You will find it in these pages. It will speak to you throughout all of Jewish tradition. Listen for it. It will ring loud and clear during the entire recovery process and help you on your way to recovery.

It is hard to give up addictions. Words do not adequately express the difficulty. There is a certain comfort in addiction and in the denial of our dependence. Usually only some severe trauma, some near-catastrophic event, makes us realize how low and desperate we have become. Listen to the words of one who wants to share:

> Even as a child I remember having problems with alcohol. For Kiddush (blessing over wine) my wine glass always had to be overflowing. One did not hold back from making a blessing, even if the overflow was drunk from the saucer. If a blessing over wine was good, a blessing over whiskey was beneficial as well. Drinking was for the sake of fulfilling another mitzvah (divine commandment), and another, and yet another. Yiddishkeit (ethnic Jewish identity) included Bronfe, Mehd and Schnapps along with wine. And what was Passover without Shlivovitz? We Jews have a rich variety of alcohol in our culture. I never thought I was an alcoholic. As a child I would pass out at a Passover Seder. But this was cute, because I was a "happy little drunk." This hap-

pened also at a Sukkot celebration or Simchat Torah or Purim. I remember as a child going around
drinking the cups left by adults at a simcha (happy occasion) in shul (synagogue). Didn't everyone do that? I had one great-uncle who ruined a
career as a talented violinist because he began to
show up at concerts too drunk to perform. We all
thought it was hilarious when we had to fish
Uncle Zalman out of the bathtub after he drank
too much at my brother's Bar Mitzvah. But Shikker was always a goy....

Jews are addicted in our community. Face it. We
have. This book is here to help. We are here to
help. Come journey to recovery with us. Together,
we will try to save your life, nothing less.

The Holy Blessed One built a Jerusalem above in the likeness of the one below but has made an oath not to enter heavenly Jerusalem until first entering earthly Jerusalem.

(Zohar 1, 80b; III, 15b)

M. GRÜNBERG

STEPPED AND
ARCHED
IN THE HILLY
OLD CITY
OF JERUSALEM

Preface by Abraham J. Twerski, M.D.
Introduction by Rabbi Sheldon Zimmerman
with Illustrations by Maty Grünberg
Afterword by the JACS Foundation

Twelve Jewish Steps to Recovery

A PERSONAL GUIDE TO

TURNING FROM ALCOHOLISM

AND OTHER ADDICTIONS

RABBI KERRY M. OLITZKY
STUART A. COPANS, M.D.

JEWISH LIGHTS Publishing
Woodstock, Vermont

Twelve Jewish Steps to Recovery: A Personal Guide to Turning
from Alcoholism and Other Addictions
copyright ©1991 by Kerry M. Olitzky and Stuart A. Copans

Library of Congress Cataloging-in-Publication Data

Olitzky, Kerry M., 1954–
Copans, Stuart A., 1943–
    Twelve Jewish steps to recovery: a personal guide to turning
from alcoholism and other addictions by Kerry M. Olitzky and
Stuart A. Copans

    1. Alcoholism–Religious aspects–Judaism. 2. Jews–Alcohol use.
3. Alcoholics–Rehabilitation. 4. Twelve-step programs–Religious
aspects Judaism. I. Copans, Stuart. II. Title. III. Title: 12 Jewish steps.

HV5185.045 1992   362.29'286'089924–dc20   91-25346
ISBN 1-879045-08-7 (cloth)
ISBN 1-879045-09-5 (paper)

First edition

10 9 8 7 6 5 4

Manufactured in the United States of America

Book and cover design by Levavi & Levavi

Illustrations by Maty Grünberg

Published by JEWISH LIGHTS Publishing
A Division of LongHill Partners, Inc.
P.O. Box 237
Sunset Farm Offfices—Route 4
Woodstock, Vermont 05091
Tel: (802) 457-4000
Fax: (802) 457-4004

Contents

Acknowledgements

Behind each word in this book are heard many voices. Some of these voices choose to remain anonymous. Others we wish to recognize and thank. While there are far too many people to mention them all by name, we do want to express abiding appreciation to our colleagues and friends at the JACS Foundation in New York City who have opened up their lives to us and taken us along with them on their journeys in recovery. In particular, we thank Jeff Neipris and David Buchholz.

Those at Hebrew Union College-Jewish Institute of Religion in New York, at the Fabrangen Community in Washington, DC, and at the Brattleboro Retreat in Brattleboro, Vermont, who labor with us in our own spiritual and clinical quests deserve special recognition. In particular, we thank Norman Cohen and Linda Jaffe; we also thank David Shneyer, Nick Belsky, Jill Gentilin, Elizabeth Reasoner, and Barbara Uhrie.

Our editor, David Szonyi, turned thoughts into words. We owe him our gratitude. We also express our gratitude for the creative insights of our colleague Lawrence Hoffman, who brought this idea to Jewish Lights. And our publishers, Stuart and Antoinette Matlins and Jevin Eagle, have helped make this labor of love soar heavenward. This volume would not be possible without them. Our words are their words.

Finally, we feel richly blessed by spouses and children who nurture our deeds and thoughts everyday that we live: Sheryl, Avi, and Jesse Olitzky and Mary, Laurie, Roy, Jon, and Ben Copans. It is because of them that our words and lives find profound meaning in this world and beyond.

RABBI KERRY M. OLITZKY
Hebrew Union College–
Jewish Institute of Religion,
New York

STUART A. COPANS, M.D.
Brattleboro Retreat
Brattleboro, Vermont

Elul 5751
August 1991

Preface

The most serious public health problem of this generation—substance abuse, which includes alcoholism and both licit and illicit drug addiction with their many and varied sequelae—is indeed a problem that poses a challenge to the Jewish community. The only reason for making this observation is the intense denial within the Jewish community, as expressed in the Yiddish aphorism, "Shikker is a goy [A drunk, a Gentile is]," a statement that has now been amply disproven. Drug addiction, whether to prescribed or "street" drugs, never did qualify for the assumed immunity, yet here too denial prevails within the Jewish community.

A further difficulty is that even when denial is finally overcome, there is much resistance to the most effective treatment modality for these conditions: the Twelve Step programs of Alcoholics Anonymous (AA), Narcotics Anonymous (NA), and their respective family groups. Reasons for resisting participation in AA and NA are legion,[1] and Jews have added a potent resistance to the list: "AA and NA are Christian programs, and Jews are not permitted to participate in them."

1

It is true that AA had its origin in the Oxford Group, who were Christian fundamentalists. However, the principles of AA and NA as presented in Twelve Steps are not in any way non-Jewish. To the contrary, all of the Twelve Steps can be found in the Talmud and traditional Torah works.

Olitzky and Copans have made a major contribution in this delightful book, wherein they demonstrate conclusively that the Twelve Steps are very, very Jewish. The material is presented succinctly and with great lucidity, and no one can claim that it is too esoteric for the layperson. After reading this book, no one can legitimately argue that the Twelve Step programs are alien to Judaism.

There will undoubtedly be those who will say, "Yes, but..." and will point to the majority of AA/NA meetings being held in church basements and the traditional recitation of the Lord's Prayer as evidence of the Christian character of these programs. It should be evident that the reason meetings are generally held in churches rather than in synagogues is precisely because the Jewish community never considered addiction to be its problem. Insofar as the Lord's Prayer is concerned, it is not an integral part of the Twelve Step program, and everyone is free to chose his/her own prayer. Some of the prayers cited by the authors in this book are particularly appropriate for people in recovery.

If there is any lingering doubt as to the universal application of the Twelve Steps, let me point out a simple fact. Under what circumstances would you ever find an *Orthodox, Hasidic* rabbi recommending without reservation a treatise on spirituality written by a *Reform* rabbi and another psychiatrist? It should be clear that if rabbis representing denominations that have major differences in their respective positions are unanimous in the espousal of the Twelve Steps, there is no conceivable reason to object to them on religious grounds.

Addictive behavior of any type, whether to alcohol, drugs, foods, sex, or gambling, is often a manifestation of maladjustment to life situations. Needless to say, there are many other types of maladjustment that are not of an addictive character. The same Twelve Steps that have proven so effective in recovery from addictions can also be helpful in avoiding or correcting other maladjustments, and Olitzky and Copan's presentation of the Twelve Steps should therefore be of value to persons who have problems that do not involve any specific addiction.

In addition to demonstrating the compatibility and indeed the Jewish character of the Twelve Steps, the authors have also elucidated them in a manner that make this book recommended reading for people of all denominations.

ABRAHAM J. TWERSKI, M.D.
Medical Director and Founder
Gateway Rehabilitation Center
Aliquippa, Pennsylvania

Introduction

My first serious encounter as a rabbi with the problem of Jewish alcoholism and Jewish alcoholics took place during my first year in the rabbinate, over twenty years ago. A member of Central Synagogue, my former congregation in New York, called on the telephone saying that she had to see me as soon as possible. We met that very day. She indicated to me that her husband was an alcoholic and that whenever she had told me and her friends that her husband was on a business trip he had actually been drying out in a rehab center. I was startled and confused. I told her that I had never seen him drink. In all the times we had been together socially or in the congregation, I had never seen him with a drink in his hand. Naively, I had asserted that he couldn't be an alcoholic. She smiled and explained that he never drank socially or at home. He only drank at work.

This brave and heroic woman was taking a risk. She had received her husband's permission to tell me the truth. She instinctively felt that I would not turn her away and that I would be responsive to a simple request she would make. She told me that there were many Jewish alcoholics and that she and her husband hoped that I would join them on a six-month voyage of discovery. They would take me to AA meetings, Al-Anon meetings, and Ala-teen meetings throughout Manhattan. They would introduce me to their acquaintances and friends in AA. If I would be willing, Jewish members of AA would come to speak with me. For six months they took me by the hand, and I received my primary lessons about alcoholism and about the extraordinary number of Jews who are alcoholics.

The rest is history. Central Synagogue was the first synagogue to host an AA group. The Federation of Jewish Philanthropies of New York established the first task force on Jewish alcoholism. Out of that task force came the retreats that led to the founding of JACS. The programs have been numerous, the impact national and international. What an extraordinary twenty years these have been.

I was privileged and blessed to be one of the first rabbis to work with, counsel, and be taught by Jewish alcoholics. In those first five years alone, I counseled and met with hundreds of Jewish alcoholics. From them I learned so much about life, about faith, and about the presence of the living God as an essential part of life. Through them, the words of prayer took on more profound significance. In their agony and in their healing, faith became a primary category.

The alcoholics I worked with came from a variety of Jewish backgrounds, some very traditional, some secular, but most from Conservative and Reform backgrounds. Most were unobservant at the time that I met with them. Interestingly, a few were Hasidic as well. Those from more liberal backgrounds talked about how unprepared they were as Jews for the faith demands and process of the Twelve Steps. They knew a lot about Jewish history and holidays, but very little about God. The synagogues and temples they attended were active places, but lacked spiritual depth and meaning in their eyes. They felt that the services left them untouched and that the rabbis preached about everything but God. I never argued with them about their perceptions. After all, their perceptions were real for them, and they were desperate for spiritual contact.

As a liberal rabbi and a liberal Jew, I find that the encounter with Jewish alcoholics and alcoholism and the Twelve Step program of AA has proven essential to my growth and becoming. Liberal Judaism as practiced in this country has often centered around ethnicity, folk traditions, social and political activism, social justice, and community philanthropy. Much of our Jewish energy has been spent in these areas. For many of us the burning fire of faith, although desired, was an unknown. We found ourselves removed from the flame of the burning bush that Moses encountered. We envied the spiritual vibrancy and passion of other movements in Judaism. For whatever reason, spirituality was not a part of our daily or weekly Jewish existence.

The beauty and significance of the Twelve Step program is that it enables us and those with whom we work to find a Jewish center of spirit and faith in our lives. Integrating the Twelve Steps with the profound teachings of Jewish tradition and faith and with the traditional process of *teshuvah* (repentance and return) enables liberal Jews to find a program that puts into an understandable and doable process the search for the world of the spirit and a personal relationship with God.

I never left a counseling session untouched by God's presence. I have stood before the Holy Ark many times as Jewish alcoholics have prayed or confessed or let go. I have wept with them, I have been angry with them, I have been enriched spiritually to the very depth of my being. I know that this has been the case with other liberal rabbis and Jews as well. We have grown far away from some of the sources of our faith. We, too, need a way back and in. That unique combination of Judaism and the Twelve Steps takes us by the hand and guides us to possibilities and affirmations of belief that few of us thought possible. We transcend all the barriers and stand at the burning bush and at Sinai once again.

RABBI SHELDON ZIMMERMAN
Temple Emanu-El
Dallas, Texas

How To Use This Book

This book requires a special kind of reading. You don't have to sit and read it cover to cover, nor even start at the beginning. Flip through the pages. Read a little at a time, over and over, if you like. Read a step a day, or a step a week, or a step a month—whatever works for you. Just read it. And get others to read it also. Together we can all find strength from the Twelve Steps and our Jewish tradition.

> Surely this instruction which I enter into covenant with you today is not too much to comprehend, nor is it beyond your grasp. It is not in heaven, to prevent you from saying "Who from among us can go to heaven and get it for us and teach it to us so that we may comply with it?"
>
> Neither is it across the seas to prevent you from saying, "Who from among us can get to the other side of the sea and get it for us and teach it to us so that we may behave in accordance with it?"
>
> No. This teaching is very close to your mouth, in your heart, so that you may observe it.
>
> *Deuteronomy 30:11-14*

The Twelve Steps
of
Alcoholics Anonymous[2]

The Twelve Steps are reprinted and adapted with permission of Alcoholics Anonymous World Services, Inc. Permission to reprint and adapt the Twelve Steps does not mean that AA is affiliated with this program. AA is a program of recovery from alcoholism—use of the Twelve Steps in connection with programs and activities that are patterned after AA but that address other problems does not imply otherwise.

1. We admitted we were powerless over alcohol —that our lives had become unmanageable.

2. Came to believe that a Power greater than ourselves could restore us to sanity.

3. Made a decision to turn our will and our lives over to the care of God as we understood Him.

4. Made a searching and fearless inventory of ourselves.

5. Admitted to God, to ourselves, and to another human being the exact nature of our wrongs.

6. Were entirely ready to have God remove all these defects of character.

7. Humbly asked Him to remove our short-comings.

8. Made a list of all persons we had harmed, and became willing to make amends to them all.

9. Made direct amends to such people wherever possible, except when to do so would injure them or others.

10. Continued to take personal inventory and when we were wrong promptly admitted it.

11. Sought through prayer and meditation to improve our conscious contact with God as we understood Him, praying only for knowledge of His will for us and the power to carry that out.

12. Having had a spiritual awakening as a result of these Steps, we tried to carry this message to alcoholics, and to practice these principles in all our affairs.

M. GRIMBERG
...STEPPED AND
ARCHED
IN THE HILLY
OLD CITY
OF JERUSALEM

Honesty

Step One

**WE
ADMITTED
WE WERE POWERLESS
OVER ALCOHOL—
THAT OUR LIVES HAD BECOME
UNMANAGEABLE**

✓ We. Not them. Us. That means we are in this together.

✓ No more denial, blaming others, pretending.

✓ Your dependency is controlling your life. It is wreaking havoc everywhere. Admit it.

✓ Dependency is a problem. Face the facts. It is messing up your life, hurting you and those who love you.

✓ This simple admission gives us the power to get on the road to recovery.

By reading these lines, you have already taken the first and most important step in recovery. All first steps are difficult. We understand that. Everyone understands that. That is why we and many people in your life are here to help.

You are following in the footsteps of our ancestors in this brave beginning. When our people were poised at the Red Sea, the Egyptian armies

15

in hot pursuit, they panicked. The Israelites were afraid to cross. Moses cajoled them, but to no avail. Fearful that they had come so far only to perish in the waters, our ancestors were ready to return to Egypt and again become enslaved. This may also be our fear. We stand at the threshold of the Red Sea every day struggling, fighting the urge to return to the slavery of our dependency.

One man arose, Nachshon ben Aminadav, a simple man, neither hero nor leader, and stepped into the raging waters. Then a miracle occurred. The waters parted, and these former slaves walked on dry land toward freedom.

You too must be willing to take the first step. Others will persuade you, even try to help you. But the miracle of recovery is not possible until you can take the first step yourself. Then the miracle of recovery will begin for you.

Our sages teach that the process of repentance, of turning and reawakening, begins with the act of seeing ourselves clearly, with all our imperfections. Our recovery begins when we give up on denial, when we admit to our powerlessness over addictions, when we see how utterly unmanageable our lives have become.

The "we" is important. Both Judaism and AA emphasize community and the support it offers each member. As Jews, we move through history as a community, in prayer, celebration, even sorrow. Remember the "bad" child of the four in the Passover Haggadah, the liturgical book used during the Passover ritual meal? That child was considered "bad," some even called him "evil" or "wicked," because he said, "God did not do anything for *me*. I was not there." But it was *we* as an entire people who went through slavery and were liberated; *we* who must remember.

Listen to the words of someone who does remember: "I'll never forget the last seder before I got help. Zeyde (grandfather) was leading us in listing aloud the Ten Plagues, and suddenly I began to see my own: alcohol, cocaine, dishonesty, neglect."

This admission is like the confessional prayers of the High Holidays. *We* ask for forgiveness for all we have done or said to profane our lives. This use of "we" binds us as a group. *We* all sinned. *We* are in this together.

Feeling part of a small group—a *minyan* (prayer quorum) or a *chavura* (extended family-like social group) in community life—is a basic human need. Perhaps you used alcohol or drugs to become part of a group. That's the past. Now you might rejoin the Jewish group. You will gain strength from it. Attend worship services regularly. Volunteer to help or serve on a committee. Whatever you do, go to a local synagogue and join in. Go to AA meetings too. Get there early. Make coffee. Set up chairs. Stay late.

Choose a sponsor and a teacher. If you really look, you'll find both. There's no real mystery to it. It may feel like a conscious choice or an inspiration. Our tradition says that "when a student is ready, a teacher will appear."

But don't just wait for it to happen. Take an active role in choosing an AA meeting, in selecting a rabbi to be your spiritual counselor, to guide you and help you find your place in the Jewish community.

Go ahead. Jump in the water; the water will recede.

We don't want to kid you. Recovery will be a difficult journey, filled with success, failure—and disappointment. Remember, it took our people forty years, an entire generation, of wandering in the desert before we were able to reach the promised land. We had to rid ourselves of the slave mentality.

With each leg of the journey there arose obstacles to be endured and overcome. You have to do the same thing. First, you shake the addiction, then the self-perception of an addict.

Since we delude ourselves into believing that we control so much in our lives and in the world, we are terrified at the prospect of not being in control. As a people, we know what it is like to feel powerless. How often have we been forced to move throughout our history, often feeling helpless to shape our own destiny.

Our grandparents! In the darkness of night, they packed their bags and fled in fear for their lives and those of their families. Yet, somehow our people always have known that they had to take the first step if they were to improve their lot. Powerlessness does not have to be passivity.

As Jews, we do not believe in chaos. Rather, order is what anchors us in this world. For countless generations, Jewish teachers have argued that the world was created according to an orderly plan.

Look out your window. The sun will rise and set each day. One season will evolve into another. Count on it. Likewise, our tradition teaches us that we are created anew each day, as is the world, giving both the opportunity to start afresh.

When the world we have built and the family we have nurtured are threatened because of our dependence, we should act. Do we have to wait until they are destroyed as a result of our addiction before we are ready to give up that to which we're addicted? No. Don't wait. Do it now. When we admit that we are powerless, that order may be restored in our lives—as part of the way the world works, and we can count on it—we begin to live again, experiencing rebirth and renewal.

As we will see in Step Two, when we are ready to trust the orderliness of the world once again, things will happen to affirm that trust.

HELP FROM OUR TRADITION

Nothing remains the same; everything blossoms, everything ascends, everything steadily increases in light and truth. The enlightened spirit does not become discouraged even when it discerns that the path of ascendence is circuitous, including both advance and decline, a forward movement but also fierce retreats, for even our retreats abound in the potential of future progress.

Rabbi Abraham Isaac Kook

SOMETHING TO THINK ABOUT

Find yourself a teacher and acquire for yourself a colleague and friend.

Pirke Avot 1:6

TOWARD SOBRIETY, A PSALM

> Your anger may last only for a moment
>> Your favor a lifetime
> Tears may linger at evening
>> but in the morning comes joy.

Psalm 30:6

TEFILLAT HA-DERECH
(prayer said upon embarking on a journey)

May it be Your will, Adonai, my God and God of my ancestors, to lead me, to direct my steps, and to support me in peace. Lead me in life, tranquil and serene, until I arrive at where I am going. Deliver me from every enemy, ambush and hurt that I might encounter on the way, and from all afflictions that visit and trouble the world.

Bless the work of my hands. Let me receive divine grace and those loving acts of kindness and mercy in Your eyes and in the eyes of all those I encounter. Listen to the voice of my appeal, for You are a God who responds to prayerful supplication. Praised are You, Adonai, who responds to prayer. Amen.

M. GRÜNBERG / ZION GATE / JERUSALEM
OPPOSITE MOUNT ZION

Hope

Step Two

CAME TO BELIEVE
THAT A POWER GREATER THAN OURSELVES
COULD RESTORE US
TO SANITY

✓ Believing in a Power greater than ourselves is a choice we make.

✓ Making this choice begins the process of recovery.

✓ At this stage it may be simple, concrete things or people that help us take this step.

*A*s Jews we may be uncomfortable when we first consider Step Two. We may hear it as claiming that we are not responsible for what happens to us, that we will be helped or saved by something or someone outside of ourselves who does it for us. Some of us even hear it as "salvation" in a Christian sense, with someone redeeming us. It can be very uncomfortable. We turn off, shut down, feel threatened

But first, we have to see that the step says "*could* restore us to sanity," not *will*. The movement from "could" to "will," from potential to actual, depends on us.

Whether or not you decide to believe in a Power that is greater than yourself is a choice that you make. You decide. We decided. And, you even get to decide—or maybe it would be better to say *have* to decide—just what that Power is.

For our part, we know that God exists. For you, that Power may be less defined, less specific, less real. But to move ahead to sanity, you simply have to take that one step that moves you outside the trap of yourself, of total self-involvement. One addict in recovery explained, "I never thought of myself as a religious person. It was because the dope was clogging my mind and my spirit." It doesn't matter whether it is God with a long white beard, or with a woman's form, a vague cloud, or anything else you can imagine. It only matters that there is something or someone there beyond and beside you. You just have to decide you want to connect with it.

When you make that decision, you have taken a step that leads you not only to God, but also to the other important people in your life—family, friends, an AA sponsor—who will also help you to restore your sanity.

When our Biblical ancestor Joseph was looking for his brothers in Dothan, he wandered, lost, until he chanced upon an unnamed person who helped him find his way. Joseph could not find it on his own. Rabbi Menachem Mendl, a great nineteenth century Hasidic rebbe, teaches that when Joseph's soul cried out from the depths of despair inside him, he was struggling to know what he really wanted and yearned for. Only by knowing this would he be able to return to his path in life. Only then would his vision actually become his path.

Like Joseph, we find ourselves confused about our life's path and so turn to alcohol, drugs, food, sex, and gambling. But even Joseph did not realize until much later in his life, after he became Pharaoh's viceroy, that neither he nor the brothers who had sold him into slavery really were in control. God had a plan for Joseph's life; he merely had to find it.

We Jews always have known that belief is essential—but that doesn't mean it is easy. If you are struggling with belief, you have lots of company now and throughout our long history. In fact, our tradition tells us, the one power God withholds even from Godself is the power to make us believe. But hard doesn't mean impossible. "Not yet" isn't never, and difficulty in faith isn't failure.

Look at the golden calf incident, where we turned our backs on God after all God did for us in bringing us out of Egypt. But God hadn't done anything for us lately. How far is it from the golden calf to the heroin addict's golden arm[4] or the compulsive gambler's lost money? Our sages knew that the distance was very short. In fact, perhaps there is no difference between the golden calf and the golden arm. The sages pointed out that there are many kinds and forms of golden calves in our lives.

HELP FROM OUR TRADITION

Abba Mieri taught in the name of the Baal Shem Tov, "For even the one who is occupied with the daily pursuits of business, when the time arrives for afternoon prayers, he hurries, sighing, praying with a broken heart. This sigh alone pierces the heavens."

SOMETHING TO THINK ABOUT

Rabbi Meir said: "Study with all your heart and with all of your soul to know God's ways and to watch at the doors of the Divine law. Keep God's law in your heart and let Divine reverence always be before your eyes. Keep your mouth from sin and purify and sanctify yourself from trespass and iniquity and God will be with you in every place."

Babylonian Talmud, Berachot 17a

A MEDITATION

Live by the commandments; do not die by them.

Babylonian Talmud, Sanhedrin 7a

TOWARD SOBRIETY, A PSALM

Fortunate is the person who has not followed
    the plan of the wicked,
      or participated with sinners.
      or joined the company of scoffers.
Rather, his desire is the teaching of Adonai,
    and he meditates on that teaching
    all the time.
He is like a tree firmly planted beside
    abundant waters
    that yields its fruit in season
    whose foliage never withers
    and whatever he does prospers.

Psalm 1:1-3

A PRAYER

In desperation, I call out to You for help and guidance through this trying, tumultuous, painful whirlwind of confusion. I find myself haunted with emotions that are unbearably ridden with guilt and endless introspective questioning of who I have become. My hungry soul is starving for the answers to satiate its craving for comfort and contentment.

The agony is no longer at a surface level but has embedded itself deep within the innermost layers of my being. The dagger of denial is piercing deeper and deeper through the confines of my essence, and the scars are becoming more difficult to conceal.

I pray for Your assistance in easing this excruciating torment that I have afflicted myself with. I must realize though, that all I can expect from You is Your guidance. I, alone, must labor to create my transformation.

The courage to change is the most trying, difficult and challenging task that has ever been set before me. I now realize that, step by step, with Your infinite love, patience and wisdom, I can take hold of the serenity I so long to grasp. With belief and trust in You, my precious God, everything is within my reach. At times, however, I must lift up my arms and outstretch my hands just a little bit further.

Esther L.
Queens, NY

M. GRINBERG / THE LIONS GATE

Faith

Step Three

MADE A DECISION
TO TURN OUR WILL
AND OUR LIVES
OVER TO THE CARE OF GOD
AS WE UNDERSTAND GOD

✓ Decisions shape our lives and determine how we grow.

✓ The very act of deciding means that you begin to take back control of your life.

✓ When you change who you are, trying to become what you might be, you enter sacred time and sacred space. There, the old you slowly evolves into the new person you yearn to become.

✓ This decision may take the form of an enormous leap. Don't be afraid to make it. It's all part of getting sober and whole again.

✓ The way you live your life, and the decisions you make, reflect your understanding of and relationship with God.

✓ As much as we think that we can go it alone, especially after a little success on the road to recovery, we find that God is truly the source of our spiritual nourishment, inspiring us to move forward.

When alcohol or drugs cloud your mind and paralyze you, distorting your decision-making ability, you no longer are in control. Once you again begin making decisions, you may hesitate, feel uncertain, make mistakes. But once you get going, it will seem like the smoothest ride you've taken in a long time.

But that good feeling also is somewhat illusory. You'll still feel plenty of bumps. When you leave the person you know so well to become the person you really want to be, it's very scary. You may well want to turn back, to return to Egypt. Don't be afraid to be frightened—it's very much part of recovery.

Some people think that faith in God comes easily: you wake up one day and BAM! it hits you. No way. For Jews, belief in God is a struggle. We spend our lives trying to figure out the range and shape of that belief, what it means, how it compels us to act.

Just start by deciding that you will try to believe. You will have doubts; we all do. You will have days when you think that God is everywhere. You might spend days thinking that God is completely hidden from the world. When you see injustices, you may be angry and defiant. Somehow, keep struggling, keep working at it. Ultimately, your belief will breathe fresh life into your soul. This is the way one friend put it, "My soul was empty and I tried to fill it with food. It didn't work."

Throughout the Jewish calendar year, we are given opportunities to start again, to make *teshuvah*, a turning, to turn toward God and the path of routine life. Yes, *routine,* nothing special, a regular life.

For the entire month of Elul (around late August or September, depending on the year), before Rosh Hashanah (Jewish New Year) and Yom Kippur (Day of Atonement), the birthing of the world and the day of ultimate decision, we prepare ourselves. We get ready for the day that each year symbolizes that moment when we shed our past and begin our journey toward personal repair. The very beginning of Scripture captures this time when fearfulness and bleakness can be transformed: "When God began to create...the world was chaotic, without order. And so, God drew near to the chaos and brought light to the world in order to illumine the darkness." (Genesis 1:1-4)

Here, at this place, you take the third step of your journey. Just as the creation of life is a process of growth, so too is the process of recovery. With each moment of living sober, free from addiction, you grow stronger, both in purpose and in resolve.

Stepping back from the canvas of creation, God recognized that the finishing touches were missing. Instead of raising again the artist's brush, God paused and handed it to us, placing the final responsibility of ongoing creation in our hands. We have much work yet to do. We are not talking about large things like mountains and rivers. No— even greater things like you and your life and the love and respect of your family and friends and colleagues. God is not going to do all the work. You are God's partner.

Get to know God, before you are ready to turn anything over. Use prayer and meditation. Create in Shabbat, the Sabbath, a place of peace and refuge for yourself. Music and poetry can help too, especially *niggunim,* the wordless chants of the *Hasidim,* orthodox Jews who passionately serve God, easily discernible by their long black coats and hanging side curls.

This adult child of alcoholics found God: "After a year and a half of therapy, I was strong enough to go to Israel and study in a yeshiva. In learning, I found the source of my light. I first started subduing my rebellious spirit to God's law. This required a trust I had barely begun to cultivate. I first tasted humility when I realized I lived in a spinning universe and could no longer tolerate it. Revelation fixed a meaning to life. For the first time ever I rejoiced in the fulfillment of a purpose."

Sometimes, we come to know God through other people. Try to be more aware of others. Listen carefully. God often speaks through those who seem least likely to be holy messengers.

Don't expect everything to happen at once. The contemporary talmudist Adin Steinsaltz once said, "Expecting too much of yourself is one way to keep yourself from doing anything." Expecting too much to happen too quickly also is a good way of blinding yourself to what actually is happening. Trees that look dormant, even dead, in winter are really preparing themselves for rebirth in spring.

Have a sense of your goal. Then, do your best to keep heading in the right direction—towards Step Four. Don't expect to get there without being aware of the journey that carried you forward, with all its hardships and wonder.

HELP FROM OUR TRADITION

At first, Adam apparently thought he was responsible for everything. Such a big burden for a person who just had been created. When the sun set on the first evening after Adam's creation, he exclaimed, "Woe is me! Because I have sinned, the world has become dark all about me; it will surely return to chaos! With this death, Heaven is punishing me!" All night he sat, fasted and wept; Eve did the same. Just as dawn was about to break, Adam said, "This is just the way things are." And he arose...

Babylonian Talmud, Avodah Zarah 8a

Prayer and communication with God takes many forms and shapes, including silence. The rabbinic interpretation called midrash emphasizes the powerful aspect of silence when contemplating God.

When God revealed Torah, no bird sang or flew, no ox bellowed, the angels did not fly, the Seraphim (ministering angels) ceased from saying, "Kadosh, Kadosh, Kadosh (Holy, Holy, Holy)," the sea was calm, no creature spoke; the world was silent and still, and the divine voice said: "I am Adonai your God..." If you are surprised at this, think of Elijah: when he came to Mount Carmel, and summoned all of the priests of Baal, and said to them, "Cry aloud, for He is God," God caused all the world to be still, and those above and those below were silent, and the world was, as it were, empty and void, as if no creature existed, as it says, "There was no voice nor any answer." (1 Kings 18:27, 29) For if anyone had spoken, the priests would have said: "Baal has answered us." So, at Sinai, God made the whole world silent, so that all the creatures should know that there is no god beside God and so God spoke: "I am Adonai your God," and so too in the days to come, God will say, "I, I alone, am the One who comforts you." (Isaiah 51:12)

Exodus Rabbah, Yitro 29:90

Jews throughout history have tried to figure out how to live the way God wants them to live. The words of Bachya ibn Pakuda, a Spanish Jew who lived in the eleventh century, may help. In his book *Duties of the Heart,* he wrote something that may direct your thoughts heavenward, help you make that decision you want to make, and move you forward to the next step:

"You know best what is for my good. If I articulate my desires, it is not to remind You, but so that I might better understand how greatly dependent I am on You. If then, afterwards, I ask You for things that are not in my best interest, it is because I am humbly ignorant. I acknowledge

that Your choice is better than mine and I give myself over to You and the Divine direction of my life."

SOMETHING TO THINK ABOUT
The one who takes on the yoke of God's will is
freed from the yoke of worldly concerns, but the
one who throws off the yoke of God's will is bur-
dened with the yoke of worldly concerns.

Pirke Avot 3:5

Make God's will your will so that God makes your
will the Divine will. Let not your will take prec-
edence over God's will so that God does not make
the will of others the Divine will in place of yours.

Pirke Avot 2:4

A MEDITATION
Strive to do the will of God with a perfect heart
and a willing soul. Efface your will even if the will
of God seems like a burden for you.

Mahzor Vitry

A PRAYER
Each day God gives us the potential to begin
again, as if reborn. As a reminder, we are thus prepared to start each day with: *Modeh ani lifanecha,
melech chai v'kayam, shehechazarta bi nishmati
v'chemda raba emunatecha.* In translation: I stand
before You, God with humble thanks. You who
empower me with every breath that I take, You,
who have faith in me, have returned my life to me,
and I will be forever grateful.

M. GRÜNFELD
THE DUNG GATE
"MENTIONED IN THE BOOK OF
NEHEMIAH" grünfeld '88

Courage

Step Four

MADE A SEARCHING
AND FEARLESS INVENTORY
OF OURSELVES

✓ You must constantly struggle to know yourself.

✓ The only way we can get at the essence of our problem is through deep inner searching. It's the only way to find the truth.

✓ This searching reveals things we may never have thought possible.

✓ Make a mental checklist. Search the surface. Then probe more deeply until you have approached the very essence of who you really are or what you have become.

For some, Step Four is terrifying and painful. Don't try this step prematurely. Use the confidence you have developed during the first three steps to sustain your work on Step Four.

The mere thought of self-examination makes us want to put up our defenses. We want to protect ourselves. Who among us wants to be exposed to the world? Searching ourselves takes great courage.

Be honest and open with yourself. Acknowledge what you have found, and move forward. But remember: only you know what you have found. You will have to do something about it—but you don't have to tell others until you are ready.

Listen to what this man told us: "As far as I was concerned, Purim (the carnival-like Feast of Lots) was amateur night. But it provided another excuse, another rationalization. 'L'chaim (For Life),' I would say, but I knew deep down that I meant just the opposite."

Take it slow. You'll get where you are going. You may be tempted to compare yourself with others—to make you feel better or to increase your pain, thinking it will somehow help. Resist this temptation. Focus on your own healing.

Take a deep breath and dig in. It's never easy to go on a fault-finding mission when you are its target. We are taught in *Tur Orach Chayim*, a Jewish legal code prepared by Yaakov ben Asher:

> Pious ones of old used to meditate and concentrate in prayer until they rid themselves of the physical. They nurtured a spiritual strength that bordered on the level of prophecy.

Try it. Choose a favorite line of sacred text and concentrate on it. Repeat it over and over until it sings like a song on your lips. Make it your own. Some possibilities:

- "In all your ways, acknowledge God." (Proverbs 3:6)
- "Wherever you go, God goes with you." (Deuteronomy Rabbah 2:10)
- "Serve God with reverence, tremble as you rejoice." (Psalm 2:11)
- "Keep me, O God, for I have found refuge in You." (Psalm 16:1)

Now, the job will be a little easier—not because there will be less to find, but because you are stronger for having done it this way. In Judaism, this is called a *cheshbon hanefesh*, literally, an accounting of the soul.

Self-examination is an important part of Jewish tradition. We set aside time each Jewish year, at the beginning and at the end, for self-reflection, for making amends.

What did you find? There are many good things to help you get back on your feet. Start with them. In *Avot de Rabbi Natan*, a kind of academy discussion based on *Pirke Avot*, (a talmudic tractate containing the rabbis' everyday wisdom), it is written: "The eye is shown only what it is capable of seeing, and the ear hears only what it is capable of listening to."

It will take some time to find out what you need to know. You probably will have to look again and again—perhaps for several days on end. And then repeat the process once more.

Don't forget: all you are trying to find is you. On his deathbed, Rabbi Zusya of Hanipol appeared afraid to face the angel of death. When confronted by his students, he remarked, "I am not afraid that God will ask me why I was not more like Abraham, Isaac, Jacob or even Moses [and we add Sarah, Rebecca, Rachel, Leah, and Zipporah]. I am afraid that God will ask me why I was not more like Zusya."

Zusya's fear also reflects ours. With the deadly support of drink and drugs, we smother our perceptions of inadequacy. We attempt to destroy the person we have decided we can never be or raise ourselves to the person we think we have to be.

Face it: you are who you are. When the drug-induced illusions wear thin, you are left with the same self you began with, somewhat diminished, requiring more chemical support each passing moment. Yet somehow we are never alone. We have the potential to be in an ongoing relationship and dialogue with God, the Holy Blessed One. This is the covenant that God made with the Jewish people, many years ago, atop a fiery mountain called Sinai.

We have to try to live our lives in the constant reflection of that covenant. Like all good relationships, it will not be perfect; at times, it will be strained. Even Moses shattered the first set of commandments. But the midrash tells us that both sets were kept in the ark of the covenant as the people traveled to the promised land.

Don't forget the shattered tablets of your life. Keep them next to the new ones that you are carving today. Let them remind you and urge you to go forward to Step Five.

AA, NA, Al-Anon, and other self-help groups can provide you with a fourth-step workbook, a detailed list of questions to answer as part of your fourth-step inventory. They focus on attitudes, responsibilities, self-worth, self-love and love for others, signs of maturity, and an analysis of character traits.

A complement to this: take out the High Holiday prayerbook, the *mahzor*, and turn to the prayers for Yom Kippur. There you will also find questions to ponder, to probe your soul.

It is not a test. You can't pass or fail. These questions are not meant to frighten or discourage you. They are simply there to offer you a renewed life, a life of spiritual renewal.

HELP FROM OUR TRADITION

Rava wrote: If people see that painful sufferings come to them, let them examine their deeds. "Let us search out our way in life and return to Adonai." (Lamentations 3:40) If they examine their deeds and find nothing, let them seek the cause in the neglect of Torah. "Happy is the person whom You instruct, Adonai, and teach from the midst of Torah." (Psalm 94:12) If they still find that this is not the reason, they may be sure these are sufferings of love. "Adonai loves whomever

Adonai corrects." (Proverbs 3:12) If the Holy Blessed One loves a person, that person is crushed by God's painful sufferings.

Babylonian Talmud, Berachot 5a

SOMETHING TO THINK ABOUT
Playing this over in our heads helps us; let it guide you through your day, as well. Rabbi Nachman of Bratzlav taught, "The entire world is a narrow bridge; the main thing is not to be afraid."

TOWARD SOBRIETY, A PSALM
Be gracious to me, O God
   in the measure of your faithfulness
   in the measure of your great mercy
   erase my transgressions.
Wash me through and through outside
   and purify me inside.
Verily I acknowledge my crime
   and am ever mindful of my offense
   against You have I sinned
   and done what is evil in Your sight.
Because it is wrong in Your eyes when it's an
   offense and right in Your judgement.
Indeed You desire truth in the hidden parts.
Teach me wisdom about secret things.

Psalm 51:3-6, 8

A PRAYER
Praised are You, Adonai, our God, and God of our ancestors. Teach us Your Torah and bring us close to You through *mitzvot*. Lead us away from sin and transgression. Let us not be tempted or disgraced. Let not our impulse to do evil overtake

us. Help us to cling to goodness and serve You. Bless us today and every day with loving acts of kindness and mercy in Your sight and in the eyes of all humankind. Praised are You, Adonai, who treats the people Israel with kindness and love.

From the morning liturgy

M. GRINBERG
THE DOUBLE GATE
(ONE OF THE PRINCIPAL ENTRANCE)
THE END OF THE SECOND
TEMPLE PERIOD

Integrity

Step Five

ADMITTED TO GOD,
TO OURSELVES,
AND TO ANOTHER HUMAN BEING
THE EXACT NATURE OF OUR WRONGS.

✓ When we ask God to listen, we are already reaching out beyond ourselves and entering into a dialogue that will lead to healing.

✓ Telling God is the easiest. God already knows— and forgives.

✓ Telling ourselves the truth is more difficult.

✓ Admitting wrongs to another person is the beginning of trust in yourself and in other people.

✓ When we recall, word for word, what we have done, the healing process will move us forward.

*I*t might seem that it should be easier to approach another human being— even one we have wronged and hurt—before approaching God. When we admit things to God, we feel them in our heart, but they have not yet been translated into our mind. God is always ready to receive us, so we first go to God. When you think the entire world has shut you out, God is always there, ready with ever-supportive, nurturing arms.

The gates of repentance always are open. "Though your sins are scarlet, they shall be white as snow." (Isaiah 1:18) Telling God what we have done wrong may be the easiest admission. Don't expect immediate results. When God listens, that is a blessing in itself.

Even for those accustomed to prayer, approaching God is a humbling experience. The Baal Shem Tov, the founder of Hasidism, has taught us that, through the power of prayer, even the least among us can communicate with God. Every out-pouring of the heart, when spoken in earnest and with devotion, is a true prayer. Every hour is an hour of prayer; every modest home and homeless shelter is a house of God. All that is needed is a recognition that we are directed to pray from our inner selves. All that is necessary for prayer is that we pray with passion and sincerity, with hearts full of joy.

It does not happen all at once. According to the rabbis, one of the effects of transgressions is the hardening of the heart. The heart becomes like a rock, solid and impermeable, feeling nothing.

When you begin to admit your wrongs to God, openings develop, like small cracks in a rock. Once your heart begins to open, these cracks begin to widen. Finally, your heart breaks open, and the head begins to know what before only the heart felt.

A friend in recovery told us, "I got clean around Hanukkah time, one day at a time. I remember as we lit the candles each night. It was my own special miracle. I didn't think I could last eight hours without a drug, never mind eight days. Today I'm working on ten years clean, still one day at a time."

Toward the end of Yom Kippur, there is an image that captures the Neilah (final) service. The sun is setting, and we feel as if it is our last chance to confess before God. Then, the shofar is sounded, and the tension that filled our bodies releases in one swift motion. We have made it through another year.

Yom Kippur. It is not just a time to catch up with family and friends, but a spiritual exercise that leaves you spent, like an exhausting physical workout. No pain, no gain.

The alphabet of sins can act as a litany or meditation for you, if you need prompting:

> ashamnu, bagadnu, gazalnu, dibarnu dofi, he-evinu, v'hirshanu, zadnu, chamasnu, tafalnu shcker, ya-atznu ra, kizavnu, latznu, maradnu, ni-atznu, sararnu, avinu, pashanu, tzararnu, kishinu oref, rashanu, shichanu, ti-avnu, ta-inu, ti-tanu.[5]

The delineation of sins is less important than the flow of words, which take us heavenward. Just say it: I admit my wrongdoing before You.

We Jews freely interpret God's time frame and willingness to allow people to return. While the Yom Kippur liturgy suggests that we have until the closing prayers of the holiday to repent, some say that individuals have until Hoshanah Rabbah, at the end of Sukkot (the fall harvest festival); others, even until Hanukkah, which falls near the winter solstice, the "darkest day of the year." All this means that basically the opportunity to reach out to God *always* exists.

If we seize it, God will meet us halfway. That you can count on. The rabbis tell of a king's son who decided to set out on his own. He traveled far from the king's palace before he grew weary, having lost his way. His funds gone, with no place to lodge, he sent word back to the King, who replied: You find the means to begin the journey home, and I will travel to meet you halfway.

But don't just "go through the motions," thinking that you can deceive God. Don't withhold details. Some things will be hard to remember. Others will be hard to forget. When you muster the strength necessary to approach God with your misdeeds, then together you and God can face the next task.

Don't worry. If you don't approach God, the Holy Blessed One eventually will call out to you: AYEKA?—"Where are you?" Listen hard. This is what God did after Adam had eaten the forbidden fruit. God went looking for Adam. God is waiting for the word: Heneini—"Here am I. I am ready for You."

Thinking that it is a good *mitzvah* (commandment) to eat and drink on the day before Yom

Kippur, an unlearned person drank himself into a stupor. He awoke late at night, too late to hear the beckoning tones of Kol Nidrei ("All our vows"—the opening prayer of Yom Kippur). Since he did not know the prayers by memory, he decided to repeat the letters of the Hebrew alphabet over and over, beseeching God to shape them into poetry and the words of prayer.

The following day, he attended the synagogue in Kotzk. After Neilah, the final prayers, the Kotzker rebbe, Menachem Mendl, summoned him. The rabbi queried the man, inquiring about his absence at Kol Nidrei. In the rabbi's presence, he confessed his transgressions, asking whether his manner of reciting the prayers ever could be pardoned. Menachem Mendl responded, "Your prayer was more acceptable than mine. Realizing the error of your ways, you uttered your prayer out of contrition—from the very depths of your being."

We have to learn to face ourselves without being harsh and overly self-critical. When we were critical of ourselves, we could not listen. It got us nowhere.

Remember all the heart-to-hearts you had in front of that early morning mirror? Yet you continued to drink and do drugs, to gamble, to eat excessively. The struggle is constant: you will have to face that mirror every single day of your life. Place it in front of you now. What do you see? Go ahead, say it. If it helps, whisper it or scream aloud. Whatever works for you is OK. Accept whatever you see. Keep doing it until it becomes part of your daily routine.

Rabbi Nachman of Bratzlav wrote, in his book about ethics and morals called *Sefer Ha-Middot,* that in meditation, people can discuss their inner turmoil with God. Individuals may forgive themselves for actions associated with personal misdeeds, imploring God to grant their fervent prayer to come closer to God. It is impossible to be a good Jew or a good person, taught Rabbi Nachman, without devoting a portion of each day to communing with God in solitude, to having a conversation with Adonai that emanates from the heart.

While you might feel that the requisite concentration is too difficult, try anyway to express your personal thoughts through words. The Bratzlaver Rebbe said: "Words are like water which falls continuously upon a rock until it breaks through."

He concludes by teaching us that in true meditation we cry out to God like a child to a parent who is about to go on a journey. There is no sadness in such weeping—only longing and yearning for return.

Are you ready? Now you have to face the people whom you have wronged. When you speak to another human being, it forces you to speak more clearly and to really hear their reaction.

By speaking to others, we hear ourselves more clearly. Here's where the Jewish tradition really differs from others. God is always there, ready to help—but won't do the work for you. Only you can confront the people whom you have chased away and say simply "I'm sorry," to "beg mechila" (ask for forgiveness). Go from person to person. Begin with your neighbor—community starts with two people.

When you admit to someone what you've done, the knowledge that only you know, that's been a heavy burden sapping your strength, is eased because it is now carried by two people instead of just one.

When we admit to ourselves the wrongs we've committed, we may feel ashamed and guilty, isolated and alienated from all humanity. By sharing these wrongs with another person, who can accept us despite our misdeeds and who respects us for our courage in sharing them, we transform these wrongs into a sacred bond, binding us as individuals, neighbors, friends.

HELP FROM OUR TRADITION
The rabbis tell a story about a young boy who could not understand why all this admission stuff was necessary. So the rabbi instructed the child to take a feather pillow and go to the village square, which he did. Next, he was told to rip open the pillow and scatter the feathers throughout the village. Happily, he made quite a mess. Feathers were everywhere. He returned to the rabbi who said to him, "Now go and gather them together—for that is what it is like to try to retrieve all of the

words you have misspoken, all of the misdeeds you have done." Understanding, the boy got down on his hands and knees to gather the elusive feathers, which he grasped to his breast, one at a time.

SOMETHING TO THINK ABOUT

Rebbe Nachman said that a human being reaches in three directions: inward to self, outward to other people, and upward to God. The real secret, taught Nachman, is that the three are one. When we are connected to self, we can reach out to others. When we reach out to others, we may come to know God.

The gates of prayer are sometimes open and sometimes closed, but the gates of repentance are always open. As the sea is always accessible, so is the hand of the Holy Blessed One always open to receive you in penitence.

Deuteronomy Rabbah 2:12

Elimelech of Lizensk taught that a person should tell the teacher who teaches him God's ways, or even a trustworthy friend, all the evil thoughts he has that are in opposition to the holy Torah, which the impulse to do evil brings into his head and heart. He should do so when studying Torah or praying, when lying in bed, or at any other time during the day. He should conceal nothing out of shame.

By speaking these matters, by giving voice to his potential to do evil, he will break the hold of the inclination to do evil so that it will have far less power to entice him on other occasions. All this is apart from the sound spiritual guidance, which is the way of Adonai, that may be received from a teacher or friend. This is a marvelous antidote to the impulse to do evil.

When Israel prays, they do not all pray at once. Rather every congregation prays by itself, first one, then another. After all the congregations finish all the prayers, the angel that oversees prayer takes all the prayers that were said in all the synagogues and makes them into a crown and places them on the head of the Holy Blessed One.

Exodus Rabbah 21:4

TOWARD SOBRIETY, A PSALM

May the presence of Adonai be felt forever.
    May Adonai be pleased with the Divine work.
God glances at the earth and it shakes.
    God touches the mountains and they tremble.
I will sing to Adonai as long as I live
    as long as I exist, I will chant hymns to God.
May my meditation be pleasing to God
    that I may go on rejoicing in Adonai
May sinners disappear from the earth
    and the wicked be no more.
Give praise to Adonai. Hallelujah.

Psalm 104:31-35

A PRAYER

May it be Your will, Adonai, our God, to station us in an illumined corner, let our heart not be sick or our eyes darkened.

Babylonian Talmud, Berachot 17a

M. GRÜNBERG
NORTHERN WALL / HEROD'S GATE

A DECORATIVE
DETAIL ADORNING
THE ORIGINAL ENTRANCE
OF THE GATE / THE
SIDE-WA

Willingness

Step Six

WERE ENTIRELY READY
TO HAVE GOD REMOVE
ALL OF THESE DEFECTS OF CHARACTER

✓ We pretend to wish away our character defects.

✓ Working to remove some part of us entirely and leave it with God may help, but that part may never go completely away.

✓ To reach the point where we are ready to give up any part of self requires great faith.

*E*very time we think that we have made it, there is more work to do. We were ready to let God do the rest. That would have been much easier, but it doesn't work that way. It takes a lot of work to remove some part of us entirely. It may not even be possible. We may have to find ways to live with, and around, it.

Our character defects define us, in a funny kind of way, and protect us at the same time. Thus, we fear that their loss would leave us as a fragment of lf, empty and vulnerable.

Gather your courage and strength and make the step work anyhow. No person or life is perfect; it only seems that way from far away. When you interact with the world, and with others, something is bound to go wrong. You just have to work harder to set it right.

When the early descendants of Adam corrupted the world, God saw fit to wash it clean. So it is with sobriety. We're at the bottom, wallowing in our own filth. We rely on God to send forth spiritual waters to cleanse us, to wash away the debris we have caused in the depths of our dependency.

Like the generation of the flood, we knew no better. Life was as we thought it should be—because it was as it always had been—or at least as good as we could remember it.

Through the intervention of a Power greater than we previously had conceived, our path toward the good life can be realigned. Our lives have been so corrupted by alcohol and drugs, by overeating and gambling, that we eagerly anticipate the torrential rains that pour down on us. It's like running out into a storm in order to get wet. As painful as these cleansing waters sometimes seem to be, we know deep inside that the rains eventually will clear and we will be restored. The skies seem to have been dark and gloomy forever. But as the rain finally breaks through the clouds, we know that the God upon whom we rely has fulfilled a promise to us. Each time we see a rainbow in the sky, we are reminded of God's promise always to help cleanse us, if we are willing to "come clean." For us Jews, the rainbow becomes a symbol of sobriety, of freedom from overeating and gambling.

God spanned it across the heavens to color the skies following its most terrible destruction, to serve as an eternal reminder of connection with us. And we recite continually in our hearts:

Baruch ata Adonai, zocher ha-brit.
Praised are You, Adonai [upon whom we rely to] remember this covenant.

The rainbow's sheer beauty can only be experienced in its full brilliance after the darkness of rainstorms. Only now, after plumbing the lowest depths of a dismal existence, do we fully appreciate its beauty.

Jewish mystics teach us that our people had to go down to Egypt and experience slavery before they could taste freedom in Canaan. This person in recovery knows how it feels: "On Yom Kippur, I would sit there with a terrible hangover, a part of me praying that God would let me live another year, a part of me hoping that God would let me die."

According to the rabbis, when a person changes, the old self dies, and a new self is born. Yet, there is an in-between stage when we are neither old nor new self. We step not directly from our old to our new self, but from old self into *nothing*.

This is one reason why so many people need a highly structured treatment program when they first begin recovery. A twelve-step program's structure provides safety and protection when you are new and naked, tender and vulnerable. Like the cocoon that protects the caterpillar during its transformation into a butterfly, the program does not control the changing. Rather, it creates the safe environment in which the new self can be born and nurtured.

What is so frightening about changing is that we find ourselves as someone else without being sure how we became that new person. People in recovery have said to us, "How strange it feels. I like who I am, but it's not really me." To help maintain some continuity in the way we see ourselves is one important reason why Step Six is essential, moving us to Step Seven.

But how do we know that change will happen? Can we be sure that we can count on our God? We're ready, but we're worried. Daily, God purifies our soul. God takes the mess that we offer and reshapes it into its pure form. What we do with it afterwards is up to us.

Here's how a friend in recovery sees it: "Faith to me means giving up the illusion of control I never had. Only my own holiness is in my hands. The disease isolates me and makes me blind. The program has taught me to slow down the panicky blur of my life and reach out to others. Judaism teaches me to trust that I always rest under God's wing. To be Jewish is to be part of the greater whole, for the promise was given to the nation as a whole. That is worth living for."

Yael I.

HELP FROM OUR TRADITION

Rabbi Alexandri said: "When you leave your things with another human being for safekeeping, even though they might have been new when they were delivered, they often are returned used and worn out. The Holy Blessed One, however, labors differently. When we leave things in God's care, all worn out and tattered, the Holy One returns them to us new. This is so obvious. A worker will work all day and come home exhausted; when asleep, the worker is at peace, since his soul is in the hands of the Holy Blessed One. At dawn, the soul returns newly created for the worker's body. Scripture teaches us, '[Souls] are renewed every morning; great is our dependence on You.'" (Lamentations 3:23)

Tehillim Rabbah 23:7

Although we follow the order as prescribed by the Great Assembly, personal prayer, as it originally existed, is still the most beneficial. Make a habit of praying before God from the depths of your heart, using your own words, in whatever language you know best. Ask God to make you truly worthy of Divine service. This is the essence of prayer.

Nachman of Bratzlav
Likutay Etzot Ha-Shem

Once a student said to his teacher, "Rabbi, why is it that God sometimes seems so far away?" The rabbi replied, "Imagine a parent teaching a child to walk. The parent does not hold on to the child. Instead, she holds her arms outstretched away from the child, and the child walks forward in between the arms of her loving parent. As the child comes forward, the parent moves away just a little. How else can the child learn to walk?"

Some say that Psalms are the heart of the Jewish soul. We find that reciting them helps us sleep, soothes us, and moves us forward. Keep a book of Psalms by your bed or on your desk. When you are wrestling with your soul, still looking for reasons to grab that bottle or pop a pill, remember that they can help you climb the heavenly ladder.

TOWARD SOBRIETY, A PSALM:

> Adonai, hear my voice when I cry out
> Take pity on me and answer me.
> Do not turn away Your servant in anger
> You have been my help.
> Never leave me, never desert me
> Adonai will care for me still.

Psalm 27:7, 9-10

A PRAYER

Consider reciting these words each morning—or whenever you feel the need for God's purifying waters to wash you clean. Traditionally, the words are part of morning prayers.

> My God, the soul which you have given me is pure. You created it. You shaped it into being. And you breathed it into me. Now guard it for while it is still in me. One day, you will take it from me, only to return it in the days to come. But as long as my soul still energizes the life that is in me. I will thank you, my God and God of my ancestors. Creator of all life. Divine One of all souls. Praised are You who returns souls to the dead.

M. GRÜNBERG
JAFFA GATE
—FRONT—

Humility

Step Seven

HUMBLY
ASKED GOD
TO REMOVE OUR SHORTCOMINGS

✓ Humbly means with acceptance of ourselves with all our limitations. No false arrogance or pride. Our humility brings us in relationship to God.

✓ You're human. We all are. By definition, we are limited. We carry our limitations with us through life. God helps us grow beyond them.

✓ Character defects do not simply vanish. With God's help, we can change.

*M*oshe Chaim Luzatto taught, in his step-by-step book about ethics, titled *Mesillat Yesharim,* that among God's loving acts was giving people the opportunity to approach the Divine in the physical world. Although you may be surrounded in darkness, far from the divine light, you can still stand before God and call out the name of the Almighty. This act alone, says Luzatto, elevates you from a lowly state to an incredible level of closeness to God, allowing you to cast your personal burdens on God.

It's tough to be humble, especially when you have lived your life by always being its center. Go ahead: approach God. Feel God's presence in your life. Request what you want. The response may not come back as you anticipated—but listen carefully.

Jews have a difficult time doing this step. Each time we think we "have it," we need to think it through again. The tradition says it best: "Pray as if everything depends on God, but act as if every- thing depends on you." We know that we can al- ways depend on God and be received, that we can ask God anything, talk about whatever we want or need. But we also realize way deep down that God does not just "remove our short- comings." Recovery would be a lot easier if that were the case.

Shortcomings have to be worked through, worked around, transcended—all with God's help. But sel- dom are they fully removed. They remind us that they are still out there, waiting to subvert our good intentions at any time, without warning, if we let them. Don't. Be on your guard. Change your way of living. Draw on the spiritual energy that God has given you, that divine spark.

Seeing our defects clearly, we feel great pain in our hearts. Don't allow those shortcomings to drag you down again and suck you dry. Fight with all you have and God will join you in the struggle. This adult child of alcoholics said it best: "I am still afraid to spin off into pain and drown, all alone. Invisible to myself, I can't imagine what God sees. I don't know why God wants me to be whole."

Look at Moses, God's main agent for over forty years. It's too easy to dismiss him as a storybook hero, larger than life. Yet, he could not even speak right. Still, God chose him to speak to Pharaoh, to lead the Jews out of their slavery and into freedom, to direct their own lives. Moses the stutterer, the stammerer.

Change the name, from Moses to that of your AA sponsor, your NA sponsor, your OA sponsor, ACoA sponsor, your Gamblers Anonymous sponsor. Your sponsor, your Moses, may not be very articulate at times, but he/she channels God's holiness for you. Don't ever forget it. Through this person who, like you, fought for—and is still trying to save—their life. Through that person who is trying to save your life, God is joining you in working on your shortcomings. According to Jewish tradition, God will only help you with your shortcomings after you have tried overcoming them yourself. You can always rely on God. But you'll find that with God's special strength in your soul, you will be able to do it yourself and not *have* to ask God alone to remove your shortcomings.

In his *Sefer Hasidim,* a book of basic concepts on Hasidism, Yehuda He-chasid shows you how to humbly approach God, letting the Holy One suffuse your spirit.

When you pray, do so with a melody that is pleasant and sweet in your own ears. That melody will direct you to pray with a special feeling, since it will lead your heart to follow the direction of your words. When you ask God for something, choose an internal melody that strengthens your heart and when you speak God's praise, choose a song that will make your own heart rejoice. Your mouth will be filled with joyous verses before God who looks directly into your heart. In such a way, you will be able to praise God and come away with overflowing love and happiness.

Don't expect your shortcomings to disappear at once. Don't berate yourself or God when you discover that you've made the same mistake once again.

"Humility." We've heard that word a thousand times, but still can't describe it. Yet it's one of Judaism's primary concepts. How can we not be humbled by God's awesome presence? We Jews cover our heads to constantly remind ourselves that as great as we think we are, there is a much greater Power. We bow the head and bend the knee in prayer to remind ourselves that God is in charge.

It's particularly important to be humble when we ask God to help us remove our shortcomings. Humility is one of the keys that opens the gates of Heaven.

An addict told us, "Before I was in recovery, I was perfect. Now, I'm better." Perfectionism often seems to accompany addiction. Even when we come to see and admit our shortcomings, we expect them to disappear immediately. People who have been sober for years still call themselves recovering alcoholics because they know that although they're better, they're not perfect. And they have to keep choosing between two directions: either recovery or relapse; those are the only choices. It is an ongoing process.

After you've been at your lowest, felt the pain, scraped the bottom of the gutter, you'd think you'd know what it is to be humble. No—not yet. Not until you have picked yourself up and begun to live again can you be humble. Sounds strange, doesn't it?

Try to be humble when you approach God. Work at it. Be straight with God. To be humble is to speak from the strength of your limitations, not to consider yourself dirt or garbage. That is not the Jewish way. Remember, everyone is created in God's image.

HELP FROM OUR TRADITION
Rabbi Bunam of Pzhysha taught: Everyone must have two pockets so that he can reach into one or the other according to his needs. In his right pocket are the words: For my sake the world was created. And in the left: I am dirt and ashes.

Rabbi Joshua ben Levi met Elijah the prophet one day and inquired of him, "When will the Messiah come?" ·

Elijah responded, "Go and ask him yourself."

"But where is he?"

"He sits at the gates of the town."

"How will I know him?"

"He is sitting among those stricken with leprosy. The others unbind all of their bandages and then rebind them all. But this one unbinds one sore at a time and then rebinds it before attending to the next one. He thinks to himself, "Perhaps I will be needed today and so I must not delay.""

Following Elijah's advice, Rabbi Joshua went to the Messiah and spoke to him, "Peace to you, my master and teacher."

The Messiah answered, "Peace to you, son of Levi."

"When will you finally come?" Rabbi Joshua asked.

"Today," came the quick reply.

When Joshua returned to Elijah, the prophet asked, "Well, what did he say?"

"He lied to me," said Joshua, "he told me that he would come today but he has not come."

Elijah gently responded, "You misunderstood. He told you: 'Today—if you will only hearken to God's voice.'" (Psalm 95:7)

Babylonian Talmud, Sanhedrin 98a

SOMETHING TO THINK ABOUT

To an earthly monarch one goes with arms over-flowing with gifts and returns empty handed. To God, one goes with empty hands and returns with a full spirit.

Pesikta Rabbati

Rabbi Yochanan and Rabbi Elazar both said "Even if a sword is on your neck, do not refrain from praying for mercy."

Babylonian Talmud, Berachot 10a

TOWARD SOBRIETY, A PSALM:

Remember Your compassion and mercy, Adonai,
    for they have existed since ages past.
Do not remember the sins of my youth and
    wrongdoing but remember me in love for the
    sake of your righteousness, Adonai.
Good and upright is Adonai, therefore God shows
    the way to sinners.
You guide the humble to justice.
    You teach the humble Your way.

Psalm 25: 6-9

A PRAYER

    You reach out Your hand to uplift
    You extend Your welcome to those returning
      in teshuvah
    It is You who taught us to confess all wrongs
      before You
    That we might stop hurting other people
    That we might be welcomed in Your presence.

Ata Noteyn Yad
from the High Holiday Mahzor

M. GRINBERG (GATES OF HULDA) JERUSALEM.

Love

Step Eight

MADE A LIST
OF ALL PERSONS WE HAD HARMED,
AND BECAME WILLING
TO MAKE AMENDS TO THEM ALL

✓ You make the list because you are accepting responsibility for the consequences of your behavior, without regard to why you did what you did or what caused you to do it.

✓ There may be many people you harmed, intentionally or unintentionally. We often harm those we love most and wish to harm least. Begin with them.

✓ Express a willingness to say that you are responsible. Say it aloud.

✓ Rehearse in your mind and in your heart how you will do whatever you can do to undo whatever you did—and anticipate the relief that will follow.

For some people, making a list sounds silly. "Why do I need a list? I know all too well whom I've hurt." A list may be too painful to write down. "It will constantly remind me of what I've done and whom I've hurt." That's the point.

Memory is central to being a Jew. Once you make a list of everyone you have hurt, you will know what you still have to do.

Lists imply order, which we constantly are trying to bring back into our lives. Some people think that there is too much order in Judaism, too many details for doing almost everything. But we Jews believe that if we follow a specific way of doing things, an order that has worked for so many for so long, we have a better chance of reaching our goal: recovery, closeness to God. Closeness to our family, friends, and self. What else could we ask for?

As Jews, we are taught that part of our task is to restore order and goodness to the world. We have a powerful compulsion to mend the world's imperfections, to make it more fair, to correct injustice, to right what is wrong. Too often, we focus on correcting other people's wrongdoings, such as fighting the injustices they've caused.

The Eighth Step prepares us to begin making the world a better place by correcting the injustice that has come from what we have or haven't done.

As Jews, there are specific times during the year when we specifically consider whom we've wronged. But don't wait until Yom Kippur. Make your list now.

Taking direction from the Yom Kippur liturgy, ask yourself: Who are the people I have hurt by doing something to them? Or by not doing something?

Whom did I harm by telling tales about them? Whom did I insult or jeer? Whom did I mislead or neglect? Towards whom was I unkind? Whom did I hurt by yielding to my addiction? To whom did I cause pain by robbing or stealing? Who was hurt by my weakness or violence?

Make your list. Next, figure out how you can begin to make up for the pain you caused. This is not moral algebra. The list may raise old resentments, hurts, angers. Don't try to crack the entire nut at once. Begin slowly.

There are some people you may have harmed out of thoughtlessness or inconsideration. They did nothing to offend or harm you. You want to make it better. This is not a bad place to begin.

You may not be ready to make amends to everyone. That's OK. For some people on your list, now is not the time to act. Just think. That's hard enough right now. When the time comes to make amends, God will provide opportunities to do so. But that can wait until you are ready for the next step.

With some people, our feelings about making amends may be hesitant, even resentful. We may still be hurt and angry and that anger may eat away at us. We'd rather rot than make amends to them!

Begin where you are, where you can. These twelve steps are a process, to be worked through again and again, each time going a little deeper into your soul. Next time, go a little farther; be willing to do a little more. Don't get stuck here because you can't yet make amends with everyone. Let the humility of Step Seven make you realize that you can't do it all and at once—but take strength and begin.

HELP FROM OUR TRADITION

Rabbi Abraham Isaac Kook wrote, "My hope is that God, in His mercy, will grant me a complete healing among the other sick persons of His people Israel, and that in His abundant kindness He will enable me to return to Him in love. Especially do I pray that He enable me to mend whatever wrong I may have committed, whether in man's relationship to God or man's relationship to man, and that He grace me with the opportunity to repay my debts.

To my great regret I do not remember all my debts in detail. But I hope that God will bestir me and remind me of them all, and that He will help me to repay them."

SOMETHING TO THINK ABOUT

One must never say to one who has repented and changed his way of life, "Remember your former transgressions."

Babylonian Talmud, Baba Metzia 58b

TOWARD SOBRIETY, A PSALM
I became Your charge at birth
   from my mother's womb You have
   been my God.
Do not keep your distance

for trouble is pressing and
there is none to help but You.
Many bulls surround me
mighty bulls of Bashan encircle me.
They open their mouths at me
like tearing, roaring lions.
My vitality is poured out
all my bones are separated.
My heart is like wax
melting within me.
My strength is dried up like a shard
My tongue sticks to my palate
You commit me to the dust of death
But You, Adonai, don't keep your
distance speed to my help.
Save my life from the sword my precious
life from the clutches of a cur.
Deliver me from the lion's mouth, from
the horns of wild oxen, respond to me.

Psalm 22:11-17, 20-22

A PRAYER

My God, keep my tongue from causing harm and my lips from telling lies about people. Let me keep silent if people curse me. Let my soul remain humble and at peace. Open my heart to Your teaching; give me the will to practice it. May the scheming plans of those who seek my harm come to naught. Yihyu l'ratzon imrei fi v'hegyon libi lifanecha, Adonai Tzuri v'Goali. May the words of my mouth and the meditations of my heart be acceptable to You, Adonai, my Rock and Redeemer.

from the end of the Amidah prayer
(the core prayer of Jewish worship, said standing)

M. GRINBERG / DAMASCUS GATE /
JERUSALEM.

ROSETTE

PINNACLES
D. G.

Discipline

Step Nine

MADE
DIRECT AMENDS
TO SUCH PEOPLE WHEREVER POSSIBLE,
EXCEPT WHEN TO DO SO WOULD INJURE THEM OR OTHERS

✓ Do it. Don't just talk or think about it. It's OK to begin with the easy ones. Just do it.

✓ Do it face-to-face if possible and appropriate. Don't have the conversation with yourself. Don't have a conversation just in your head.

✓ Some things that we do have consequences that cannot be undone. There are also things we cannot yet bring ourselves to do. But, If you can't fix whatever it is, go fix something else.

✓ Move forward in recovery and do whatever you can do to transform the pain into peace. Experience the release. But be careful not to become someone whose apology gives personal release while causing more pain.

"There is a time to act," says *Ecclesiastes*. Now is the time. For us Jews, the deed is more important than the thought; who we are is equal to what we do. Not what we think or say we will do. Wonderful thoughts do not repair the world; small deeds begin to do so.

Making amends may be difficult. The first time may be terrifying. But going to someone and simply saying, "I'm sorry" gets easier each time you do it. So get out and go do it. Be ready to listen to someone tell you how hurt they are and how angry they were. Just ask them what you can do to try to make things right.

Of course, you're afraid to do it. Just as denying your addiction did not make it go away—it simply let you pretend that things were fine and made you feel continually worse—so your failure to make amends magnifies your sense of emptiness, imperfection, being fatally flawed.

You had to face the pain of addiction to begin on the road to recovery, and you had to share the Fourth Step inventory with someone else before beginning to correct your character defects. So now you must seek forgiveness from those you have harmed before beginning the task of rebuilding your world.

Go out and do what you have to do. But, be careful. Don't add insult to injury by trying to repair something for your sake—rather than for the sake of the person you hurt. Whatever you do, do it *l'shem shamayim,* for the sake of heaven.

Sometimes, the process will be surprisingly easy. You simply apologize and the other person is so relieved to see that you have changed, he just accepts your apology. Others will not be so forgiving. Don't let them renew your anger or your guilt. Take charge of the process.

But you are not responsible for the results. Making amends to some people may, in a peculiar way, cause more pain by opening up healed wounds. Talk about this dilemma with a trusted friend or your sponsor.

Amends can also be made indirectly. If you have stolen, repay your debt or return it anonymously. Or give *tzedakah* (a charitable donation) as amends for people from whom you have stolen whom you can't find or never knew.

Making such amends simultaneously heals ourselves and the world. By fully participating in personal recovery, we begin to actively restore *shalom,* unity and wholeness, to the world.

HELP FROM OUR TRADITION

If your deeds exceed your good intentions, your good intentions endure. But if your good intentions are more plentiful than your good acts, then your good intentions do not endure.

Pirke Avot 3:9

They asked wisdom, what shall be the punishment of the sinner? Wisdom answered: Evil pursues sinners (Proverbs 13:21). They asked prophecy. It replied: The soul that sins will die (Ezekiel 18:4). They asked Torah. It replied: Let him bring a sacrifice (Leviticus 1:4). But then they asked God and God replied: Repent and obtain atonement, my children. What do I ask of you? Only to seek me and live.

Pesikta d'Rav Kahana 24:7

SOMETHING TO THINK ABOUT

Repentance makes an individual a new creature. Previously a person may be dead through sin, now he is fashioned afresh.

Psalms Rabbah

TOWARD SOBRIETY, A PSALM

Adonai is my shepherd
  I lack nothing
God gives me my ease in rich pastures,
Leads me to take my drink by tranquil waters
Redeems my life
Leads me in the ways of right.
Out of sheer graciousness
Though I go through the gloomiest valleys
  I fear no misfortune for You are ever with me,
Your sustaining staff is what relieves me of my
  anxiety.
My enemies do not bother me because You
  are watching over me.
You have made my heart fat with richness
  my cup oozes.
As long as I live my tracks will be accompanied
  by graciousness.
I will dwell in Adonai's
  house as long as I live.

Psalm 23

A PRAYER

Before a person is healed, he must
acknowledge his illness.
Before a person finds light, she must
know her own darkness.
Before a people is forgiven, it must
confess its sins.
We confess our sins and those of our
fellows for we are responsible, one for
the other.
Heal us, Adonai, and lead us through
darkness to light.

from the Yom Kippur confessional

M. GRÜNBERG / SINGLE GATE / JERUSALEM

Perseverance

Step Ten

✓ Take pride that you are continuing, not beginning. Recovery is a process. Ongoing. It never stops.

✓ Build a habit of self-reflection in approaching everything that you do.

✓ You will slip and fall, but as soon as you realize you have done wrong, be quick to admit it. Don't wait for others to point a finger.

*O*nce you have started, don't stop. Recovery is like breathing. If you want to stay alive, you have to do it. Go easy. Establish a rhythm that works for you. You may want to begin at night to prepare yourself for the next day. Or take periodic reviews during the day. Some even find it helpful to do a "reality check" once an hour, on the hour.

In Judaism, there is a tradition to arise early to do a mitzvah. Make it right early in the morning. As a result, your entire day will be more tranquil.

Use the rhythm of the Jewish day—three times of prayer—to stop and review your behavior. Cease your usual activities. Step out of yourself and look at things the way God might look at them. Use Shabbat to review your week, to take a step back and see how far you've come (not just how much farther you have to go). Measure your time by the sacred signposts of our tradition: rituals, festivals, holidays.

However you decide to do it, set aside time each day and each week to review what you have done and what you have said. (We call these "Sabbath moments," time to pause, reflect, and gain strength to move forward in recovery.) But don't wait for Shabbat to make amends for when you have erred and temporarily have lost your footing. As soon as you realize that you are wrong, admit it. Stop everything. Step back and look at yourself objectively. Bachya ibn Pakuda taught that "Days are scrolls. Write on them what you want remembered."

Prior to the High Holidays, we take inventory and make amends. But once a year is not enough. The goal is to be able to step back from everything we do and look at ourselves objectively. Few among us can really do that. We find it helpful to develop a regular routine for taking our personal inventory.

As Jews, we pray for the messianic era, but realize that, until it arrives, our task is to make the world a place ready for messiah. Actually, Shabbat provides us with a window into the messianic era.

We all long for that time when peace and tranquility will pervade the world, and so we work all week to get a glimpse of it for such a short time.

The process of recovery is lifelong—we can't say that enough. As Jews, we are expected to take inventory and make amends. The Jewish tradition teaches that we are not required to finish the work, but neither are we free to desist from it. But we are not just Jews. We are addicted Jews who slip easily into denial; into a certain blindness, grandiosity, or perfectionism; into a failure to listen carefully enough to what others say.

That's why this step instructs us to take inventory again, even though we did it once in Step Four, to establish a continuous process. But Step Ten is different from Step Four. There we just took a moral inventory. Here we monitor our recovery. The inventory and the action to correct any wrongdoing becomes one and the same, simultaneous. One can no longer exist without the other. One friend told us, "Recovery did not prevent me from making mistakes. It made me recognize them sooner after I had made them."

HELP FROM OUR TRADITION
When good people give up their integrity to do what is wrong, they die; in doing that wrong, they die. When evil people turn away from this death to do what is right and just, they actually save their lives. When they recognize all their sins and turn away from those sins, they live and do not die. Yet, the house of Israel objects: The way of

Adonai is unjust. "Is it My ways that are unjust, O house of Israel? I will judge each one of you by what you do," says Adonai. "Return and turn away from all your sins or your iniquity will be your downfall. Throw off all the burdens of past sins. Make yourself a new heart and a new spirit. House of Israel, why should you die? I take no pleasure in the death of anyone," says Adonai. "Just repent and live."

Ezekiel 18:26-32

SOMETHING TO THINK ABOUT
It is not your responsibility to fully complete the work of repair, but neither are you free to cease from doing it.

Pirke Avot 2:16

TOWARD SOBRIETY, A PSALM
Search me, God, and know my heart
Test me and know my thoughts
See if the path to despair is yet within me
and lead me in the path of eternity.

Psalm 137: 23-24

A PRAYER
Listen, Adonai, for I am in distress. My spirits are troubled. My heart is turned within me, for I have grievously rebelled. In the street the sword is bereft, in the house it is like death. May you bring the day (of my return)...for my sighs are many and my heart faint.

Lamentations 1:20-22

M. Grinsberg
THE NEW GATE
JERUSALEM
WEST SIDE

Illumination

Step Eleven

SOUGHT
THROUGH PRAYER AND MEDITATION
TO IMPROVE OUR CONSCIOUS CONTACT WITH GOD
AS WE UNDERSTAND GOD,
PRAYING
ONLY FOR GOD'S WILL FOR US AND
THE POWER TO CARRY THAT OUT

✓ Don't wait for inspiration; look for it. You are the seeker. It's still up to you.

✓ Use whatever means you can to make a contact with God. Make a commitment to pray, meditate, and talk in your own special voice. Doing it is much more important than how you do it.

✓ Once you have allowed God to enter into your life, build a relationship of understanding.

✓ Seek to understand the dimensions of your relationship with God and of God's relationship with you.

✓ Pray for inspiration and the strength to do what you have to do.

Judaism teaches that we can come into contact with God through any activity done with the right intent—repairing shoes, weeding a garden, waxing the car, even paying our taxes! Since God is present in all things and all people, we can come into conscious contact with God through any of our interactions with the world. Through these interactions, we become aware of God's presence in our lives. One of the best ways of coming into contact with God is through prayer and meditation.

Communication with the Divine is possible through many types of expression. For most of us, who are not great speakers, we rely on others' poetry to reach out to God. Joseph Albo, in *Sefer Ha-Ikkarim* taught:

> In prayer, you gather the strength of dedication for life, allowing this life to become the fulfillment of the Divine will, the furthering of Holy purpose—a contribution to the success of that purpose, which God has established for all humanity and for the people Israel. Thus, the flavor of all prayer is the resolution which infuses the entire person and unites all of you to serve God through living.

Call together all your powers of concentration. Remove all distracting thoughts from your mind so that, when you pray, your thoughts are focused. Were you speaking to an earthly monarch, you would be extremely careful with your words, painstakingly choosing each one, so as not to say anything wrong. When you pray, you are speaking before the Holy Blessed One. Therefore, concentrate even more; God probes all thought. Before God, thought is the same as speech.

Both prayer and meditation are ways of coming into contact with God, of getting in touch with the Divine will. In some ways, these two approaches correspond to two different ideas about God. Mystics generally see God beyond the limits of our physical world. They direct their prayers and thoughts outward. Others see God as deeply within us, in that place where our will commingles with God's will. They see prayer and meditation focused inward, helping us to look deeper into ourselves.

Jewish meditation is very simple. Set aside time each day to talk with God. We find it helpful to speak out loud in a quiet voice, in a quiet place and in solitude. Some people have a special area where they most easily come into contact with God. Try different ways and places until you find your own. Treasure it and use it.

Just as it is important to call your sponsor when you don't need help, so that you can call her when you do, make contact with God when everything seems fine. If you do, in those troubled times when you feel most alone, you will know that God still is there, ever ready to listen.

Listen to the words of someone involved in the struggle to keep sober:

I am one of God's people, and one who has been chosen to find recovery. Thanks to the Twelve Step path I have begun to understand God's will for me, and never again can I claim ignorance of my actions. Yes, I will stray from the path from time to time. I am an imperfect creature of body and spirit. Nevertheless, God's will for me is simple: Just do the right thing.

As a Jew, I believe that God asks only one thing from me. God asks that I show my love; and God gives me opportunities to prove that love.

HELP FROM OUR TRADITION

Where does God dwell? This was the question with which the rabbi of Kotzk surprised a number of learned students who happened to be visiting him. They laughed, "What a thing to ask. Is it not written, 'The whole world is a manifestation of God's glory?'" Then the rabbi answered his own question: "God dwells wherever people allow the holy to fill their lives."

The Maggid of Meziritch taught in his book on mysticism Esser Orot "When one studies and prays with fear and love, that individual gains much from it. He becomes bound in his thoughts to the Creator, blessed be God. Such a worshipper sees nothing and hears nothing except the divine vitality that is in all things. For everything is from God; it is only clothed in different garments."

A MEDITATION FOR TIMES OF WEARINESS AND DESPAIR:

The people of Israel say, "We are poor. We have no sacrifices to bring as an offer." God replies, "I need only your words, as it is written, 'Take with you words [of Torah].'" (Hosea 25:2) God replied, "Weep and pray, and I will receive you."

Shemot Rabbah 38:4

TOWARD SOBRIETY, A PSALM:

Listen to my words, Adonai,
Consider my inmost thoughts
My Sovereign God, hear my voice
  To You alone do I pray
Adonai, hear my morning prayers
  I lay them before You in
  anxious anticipation.

Psalm 5:1-4

A PRAYER FROM SOMEONE IN RECOVERY:

Blessed art Thou, oh Lord,
  every day,
Because every day is precious,
Every day is a lifetime
  mirroring all life itself.
Thank you for the morning
  when I feel fresh and young
And wake to the beauty
  all around me.
Thank you for the afternoon
  when the sun is high
Suspended in triumph
  above a work-a-day world.
Thank you for the evening when
  the shadows cast a sheltering
  palm above the universe
Permitting it to pause
  ready for the dark.
Thank you for the night
  with the ever-present stars
To remind me that darkness
  is never absolute.
Thank you for the calm
  that is restorative,

Not a mindless obliteration
   of reality.
Thank you for the sleep
   that heals and strengthens
And fills my heart with hope
   for a new tomorrow.

Marcia H.

M. Grinberg / THE GOLDEN GATE / JERUSALEM

Service

Step Twelve

**HAVING HAD
A SPIRITUAL AWAKENING
AS A RESULT OF THESE STEPS,
WE TRIED TO CARRY THIS MESSAGE TO ALCOHOLICS
AND TO PRACTICE THESE PRINCIPLES
IN ALL OUR AFFAIRS**

✓ Once you've had it, it's yours forever. It may not feel near all the time, but it's never very far away. You have to reach for it.

✓ Being alive physically is no longer enough. There is so much more to life. Acknowledge your rebirth and renewal by living life fully.

✓ Share the message. Help others find the path to recovering that these steps gave to you. Preaching is good. So is teaching. But teaching and preaching by working the program is best of all.

✓ Let these insights influence all that you do

✓ This spiritual awakening will affect your work, play, eating, sleeping, and many other activities that you do not think of as spiritual.

✓ Carry the message to anyone who is in need and needs to listen: alcoholics, addicts, overeaters, gamblers, codependents, and everyone else.

Yes. You have reached the final step in your recovery—an awesome experience. Now these steps have become part of your everyday routine; they are now part of you. You are unable to distinguish where the steps end and you begin. More than that, your Judaism has been renewed through these steps. Work them again and again. Just as each Passover we are back in Egypt again as slaves, so each time we rework a step, we confront our addiction anew.

Now take what you have learned and reach out to someone else in need. It's the only way to go further. It helps both of you. And remember the further forward you go, the further from your addiction you'll be. This friend in recovery said to her sponsor, "How can I ever thank you?" The reply, "Just carry the message, carry the message."

Yet, it's important to concentrate on your own practice of the Twelve Steps before you carry its message to others. Teaching and practice. Our rabbis said:

> Regarding the person who learns in order to teach, Heaven will allow that person to continue to learn and to teach. But concerning the one who learns in order to practice, Heaven allows that person to learn and teach, observe and practice.
>
> *Pirke Avot 4:5*

Practicing these principles—honesty, taking responsibility for our actions, making amends when appropriate, and promptly admitting to others when we are wrong—helps us maintain our sobriety and carry the message to others in the most powerful way possible: through personal example.

At first, you may be shy when it comes to talking about your recovery or your relationship to God through Judaism. It takes time. But it's important to talk about the Twelve Steps in the context of Torah. Listen to the words of our tradition: "If three have eaten at the same table and have not spoken words of Torah, it's as if they had made sacrifices to dead idols." God's will is not in their thoughts. "But if three have eaten at the same table and the words of Torah were spoken, it's as if they had eaten at the table of Adonai." (Pirke Avot 3:3)

As a reentry point in Judaism, as a vehicle to mitzvot (divine commandments), let them begin to inform all of what you say, what you do, and how you live. We have accepted the mission to be "a light to the nations." Now go and bring others on the journey with you.

HELP FROM OUR TRADITION
How did Zusya bring a person to repentance? He went down all of the steps until he reached the other person's level. Then Zusya bound the roots of his soul to the roots of the other person, and together their souls did repentance.

SOMETHING TO THINK ABOUT

Said the Leover Rebbe: If someone comes to you for assistance and all you say to him is "God will help you," you become a disloyal servant of God. It is for you to understand that God has sent you to aid the needy and not to refer him back to God.

One who prays for merely his own needs is like one who works to strengthen his home alone, and does not want to help the people of his land strengthen the walls of the city. Even though he expends much effort, he remains in danger. But one who includes himself with the community expends little and remains safe.

Yehuda Halevi
The Kuzari

The difference between one who prays and one who does not pray is not to be found in the fact that the former sets aside time everyday for his prayer, while the latter does not. There is a more basic dichotomy. The types of lives those two people live are thoroughly different. The time devoted to prayer makes an impression upon every aspect of the entire day.

Abraham Isaac Kook
Olat Reiyah

A number of unbelievers lived in Rabbi Meir's neighborhood. This used to really bother him. He was so annoyed that he wanted to pray for them to die. Meir's wife Beruriah advised him, "Do not pray for an end to sinners, but an end to sin. Pray that they repent."

Babylonian Talmud, Berachot 10a

A PSALM:

of despair I called to

e.

to my pleading
keep track of sins
?
rgiveness,
held in awe.
Adonai
soul has hope
and for Your word I wait.
My soul waits for Adonai
More than watchmen for the morning
Waiting for the sunrise
Israel, hope is in Adonai
for which Adonai is continuous love
and Your great redeeming Power
It is You who redeems Israel
from all their sins.

Psalm 130

A PRAYER

Praised are You, Adonai our God, Sovereign of the Universe who makes a distinction between holy and profane, between light and darkness, between Israel and the nations, between the Sabbath and the six working days. Praised are You, Adonai, who makes a distinction between holy and profane.

from the Havdalah liturgy,
which separates Sabbath and the holidays
from the rest of the calendar

The conclusion of true *teshuva,* returni[n]
Source in Heaven, is not self-rejection or r[e]
but the healing that comes from telling our[s]
the truth about our real intentions and fin[al]
self-acceptance. This does not mean that we a[re]
now proud of who we were or what we did, bu[t]
it does mean that we have taken what we did
back into ourselves, acknowledged it as part of
ourselves. We have found its original motive, realized how it became disfigured, perhaps beyond
recognition, made real apologies, done our best
to repair the injury, but we no longer try to reject
who we have been and therefore who we are, for
even that is an expression of the Holy One of Being.

We do not simply repudiate the evil we have
done and sincerely mean never to do again; that
is easy (we do it all the time). We receive whatever evils we have intended and done back into
ourselves as our own deliberate creations. We
cherish them as long-banished children finally
taken home again. And thereby transform them
and ourselves. When we say the vidui, the confession, we don't hit ourselves; we hold ourselves.

Lawrence Kushner
God Was In This Place and I,
i Did Not Know

On Simchat Torah we finish reading the Torah
and begin again. The same is true with the
Twelve Steps. It has been said that one can only
work Step One all the way through. One works
the other steps partially, a little each time, and
must work them again and again.

Like Torah, the Twelve Steps represent an ongoing way of life, not a one-time experience.

Like Torah, the Twelve Steps experience is never complete.

As we work through and try to live by the Twelve Steps, as we study and are guided by the teachings of Torah, we grow spiritually. Each time we return to a particular Torah portion or to a different step, we see it from a different vantage point, peering further and deeper into Torah and ourselves.

Each week we concentrate on one Torah portion, but consider the entire Torah. Likewise, we work on all Twelve Steps all the time, although at any given time, we concentrate on only one.

A hint: if you have trouble with a particular step, don't skip it or beat your head against it. Go back and work through the earlier steps until you feel comfortable tackling the one that is causing you problems. And then begin again.

A PRAYER
In Judaism, we celebrate new beginnings with this prayer of thanks. *Baruch ata Adonai Eloheinu Melech ha-olam shehechayanu, vekeyimanu, vahigianu laazman hazeh.* Praised are You, Adonai our God, Sovereign of the Universe who has sustained us and brought us forward so that we might reach this day. Amen.

Endnotes

[1] Twerski, M.D., Abraham J., *How to Respond, "AA Is Not For Me"* (Aliquippa, PA: Gateway Publications, 1986).

[2] We have quoted here the original AA language, which uses the masculine pronoun in referring to God. Like many other Twelve Step programs, we avoid pronouns that refer to God, who we believe incorporates—and transcends—the characteristics attributed to both sexes.

[3] God is known by many names in Jewish tradition. Since we really do not know how to pronounce God's essential name, we generally use Adonai (literally "Lord") to refer to God.

[4] The addict spends so much money on drugs pumped into his/her arm that it is as if the arm is made out of gold.

[5] We have trespassed, dealt treacherously, and robbed. We have spoken slander, acted perversely, and wrought wickedness. We have been presumptuous, done violence, and have lied. We have counseled evil, have spoken falsely, and have scoffed. We have revolted, provoked, and rebelled. We have committed iniquity, transgressed, and oppressed. We have been stiff-necked, done wickedly, and corrupted. We have committed abominations, gone astray, and led others astray. (From the Yom Kippur liturgy)

Moving From Here to Recovering: An Afterword

On a Sunday morning in October, Jews are weeping in the social hall of a fading resort in the Catskill Mountains. For the more than 200 recovering alcoholics, addicts, and their loved ones in attendance, the tears of shame and remorse have vanished. On this final day of the autumn JACS Retreat they are shedding tears of gratitude. Many have begun to relate to their Jewish identity and are letting go of feelings of alienation and ostracism from the community. There is the growing sense that the lifeline many discovered in a church basement is a fundamental part of their Jewish heritage, a discovery of wholeness and connection with a tradition that, for some, had lost its meaning and, for others, had little meaning at all.

Rabbi Olitzky and Dr. Copans have made a significant contribution to articulating the bond of Judaism and recovery. They put to rest once and for all the misconception of many that the Twelve Step recovery process is not compatible with Jewish tradition and belief. Most importantly, they make a substantial dent in the wall of denial that has plagued the Jewish community concerning the problem of substance abuse. This is a life-saving contribution, and many will be forever in their debt.

Their work underscores the advocacy role of the JACS (Jewish Alcoholics, Chemically Dependent Persons and Significant Others) Foundation—that the disease of addiction can happen to Jews and that the age-old myth of Jewish immunity has hindered social service agencies, lay leadership, and the rabbinate from addressing the problem in an emphatic way. Under the prescient auspices of the UJA-Federation of Greater New York and United Way of New York, JACS has been endeavoring to dispel the myths, to dissolve the indifference and neglect by training, sensitizing, and speaking out within the Jewish community. Additionally, by providing programs for Jews recovering from alcoholism and chemical dependency, JACS has offered an opportunity for spiritual renewal and healing, an endeavor that has served as a model for an ever-growing number of grassroots organizations across the country.

Since the first Retreat in 1979, JACS has strived to provide an environment where Jewish self-discovery is accessible for all. The Retreat program, developed by the JACS membership, has no religious agenda, nor is one particular perspective represented as more praiseworthy than the next. Here the unaffiliated and the ultraorthodox come together as travelers on a similar journey. Though they may have embarked from different starting points, they share the same elusive destination of Jewish spiritual fulfillment. This is Judaism at its most vital and expansive, an attitude shared at the gut level by all the participants, ripened by their experiences in the Twelve Step recovery fellowships of

Alcoholics Anonymous, Narcotics Anonymous, Adult Children of Alcoholics, Al-Anon, and many others.

One cannot overemphasize the efficacy of the Twelve Step recovery movement. It is the focal point from which any serious discussion about long-term, successful abstinence from alcohol or drugs must derive. For family members, the Al-Anon and Nar-anon programs offer the most enduring means for developing healthy skills for coping with both active and recovering substance abusers. Indeed, the success of the "anonymous" programs has been so substantial, there are no reputable rehabilitation facilities that do not make attendance a mandatory component of the treatment process.

Nevertheless, it needs to be mentioned that confusion and misconceptions still abound. The success of Alcoholics Anonymous has spawned more than two hundred recovery programs, addressing a wide array of personal problems and concerns. The growing number of these op-portunities has led in recent years to much media at-tention and intellectual scrutiny. Many of the re-sulting generalizations not only betray a lack of personal experience but a profound mis-understanding of the differences between self-help and self-pity, surrender and disempowerment, spir-ituality and religion, community and cult, or healing environment and therapeutic milieu. In truth, for the millions whose lives have been saved by Alcoholics Anonymous, it is much like grumbling about a speeding ambulance because it disrupts traffic.

These issues need to be addressed because this misinformation does a tremendous disservice to those in need of help. Addiction is a disease of denial, and the addict is usually the last to acknowledge his or her dependence. At the same time, rationalizations proliferate about seeking assistance. For most, the prospect of attending an AA meeting is tantamount to a deathbed confession, the last stop on a road of broken promises and diminishing self-respect. The confusion about religion and spiritual recovery is a particularly difficult roadblock, and, for Jews in need, a long history of community ignorance and indifference about the self-help program has made it especially troublesome.

Simply put, AA works. It works for everyone, regardless of background, who is willing to be completely honest about their drinking problem. The cornerstone of Alcoholics Anonymous, to use the primary example, is the fundamental philosophy of one drunk helping another, of a community of alcoholics who, as a result of their common problem, are able to share their experience, strength, and hope in the mutual desire to stay away from a drink one day at a time. This connection, this reaching out, is available 24 hours a day. The typical AA meeting emphasizes this openness. Occasionally there are tears. Sometimes anger. Yet it is a safe environment. Everyone understands. Here the only requirement for membership is a desire to stop drinking. Some meetings are held in church basements. Yet everyone, regardless of denomination, is welcome. Religious, cultural, or economic differences are simply not on the agenda. Most groups conclude the meeting with a prayer. But the intent is a communal expression of gratitude, not dogma, nor is a belief in God, or any other philosophy, a requirement for full participation. Some members augment their recovery with therapy. Others do not. But most are paying very close attention to how they can make their lives whole once again. At the center of this self-scrutiny are the Twelve Steps of recovery, and they, too, are not an obligatory part of the program. They are suggested as an opportunity for self-awareness and peace of mind. They are experiential and, over time, can become a natural expression of one's daily life. Most importantly, they are a foundation for continued growth. As Bill W., cofounder of Alcoholics Anonymous, once noted, "AA is a spiritual kindergarten." Whether one's personal development takes the form of religious renewal or psychological and spiritual insight, the intent is for ongoing and lifelong self-expansion.

The Twelve Steps emphasize spiritual and personal awareness, taking stock, reaching out to others in need. These are basic Jewish values, and they need to be exercised much more forcefully by the Jewish community in dealing with the problem of alcoholism and chemical dependency. Addiction is a disease, not a *shonda* (disgrace) and our priorities should demand action, not statistics, emphasis on remedies rather than bemoaning reasons why. Rabbi Olitzky and Dr. Copans have offered a thought-provoking guide for the growing number of people who are seeking to enhance the recovery process from the perspective of Jewish tradition and belief. At the JACS Foundation we will continue to strive to see that more Jews be given that opportunity, that those who still suffer from addiction will find the resources they need within a community kindled by an age-old legacy of healing, compassion, and care.

JEFF NEIPRIS, EXECUTIVE DIRECTOR
DAVID BUCHHOLZ, PRESIDENT
The JACS Foundation
New York, NY

A Final Prayer

May you live to see your world fulfilled
May your destiny be for worlds still to come
May you trust in generations past and yet to be

May your eyes shine with the light of holy words
And your face reflect the brightness of the heavens
May your lips ever speak wisdom
Your fulfillment be in justice
Even as you ever yearn to listen to the words of
The Holy Ancient One of old

May your heart be filled with intuition
And your words be filled with insight
May songs of praise be upon your tongue
Your vision straight before you
Even as you ever yearn to listen to the words of
The Holy Ancient One of old

Babylonian Talmud, Berachot 17a
translated by Lawrence Kushner

For Further Help

(and to find a local group in your community)

Al-Anon Family Groups, Inc.
Intergroup
200 Park Avenue South
Room 814
New York, NY 10003
212/254-7236

Alateen
Intergroup
200 Park Avenue South
Room 814
New York, NY 10003
212/254-7236

Alcoholics Anonymous World Services, Inc. (AA)
Grand Central Station
Box 459
New York, NY 10163
212/870-3400

Cocaine Anonymous (CA)
6125 Washington Boulevard, Suite 202
Culver City, CA 90232
310/839-1141

Pills Anonymous
P.O. Box 248
New York, NY 10028-0003
212/874-0700

Families Anonymous
P.O. Box 3475
Culver City, CA 90231-3475
800/736-9805

Gamblers Anonymous
New York Intergroup
P.O. Box 17173
Los Angeles, CA 90017
213/386-8789

JACS Foundation, Inc.
(Jewish Alcoholics, Chemically Dependent Persons
and Significant Others)
46 West 58th Street
New York, NY 10019
212/397-4197

Narcotics Anonymous (NA)
World Services Office
P.O. Box 9999
Van Nuys, CA 91409
818/997-3822

**National Council on Alcoholism and Drug
Dependence (NCADD)**
12 West 21st Street, 7th Floor
New York, NY 10010
212/206-6770

National Self-Help Clearinghouse
25 West 43rd Street, Room 620
New York, NY 10036
212/642-2944

Nicotine Anonymous
P.O. Box 591777
San Francisco, CA 94159-1777
415/752-2230

Overeaters Anonymous
117 West 26th Street, Suite 2W
New York, NY 10001
212/206-8621

Sexaholics Anonymous
P.O. Box 300
Simi Valley, CA 93062
818/704-9854

Sex and Love Addicts
P.O. Box 650010 / 437 Cherry Street
West Newton, MA 02165-0010
617/332-1845

Survivors of Incest Anonymous
P.O. Box 21817
Baltimore, MD 21222-6187
410/282-3400

Glossary of Important Words and Concepts

Adonai: God is known by various names in Jewish tradition. Adonai (literally "Lord") is used to refer to God since we do not know how to (and dare not to) pronounce God's essential name

cheshbon hanefesh: a probing inventory of the soul, taken by individuals especially prior to the High Holidays

covenant: the agreement established some 3200 years ago between God and the people of Israel at Sinai

Elul: the month prior to the High Holidays (usually late August to early September), which focuses on introspection, repentance, and renewal

mitzvah/mitzvot: divine commandments given by God to the Jewish people

shalom: wholeness and completeness, epitomized by peace

teshuvah: literally a turning toward God and a righteous, religious way of life; in a broader sense, this represents returning and moving toward recovering

tzedakah: charitable giving usually of substance but also of self

Yom Kippur: Day of Atonement, according to many the holiest day of the year, this Holy Day is also called the Sabbath of Sabbaths. More than any other time on the Jewish calendar, it epitomizes the focus of introspection, repentence, and renewal

Selected Readings

Addiction in the Jewish Community
Stephen Jay Levy and Sheila Blume
Federation of Jewish Philanthropies
New York, New York

As a Driven Leaf
Milton Steinberg
Behrman House
West Orange, New Jersey

Beggars and Prayer
Adin Steinsaltz
Basic Books
New York, New York

The Book of Psalms
A New Translation
Jewish Publication Society
Philadelphia, Pennsylvania

The First Jewish Catalog
Richard Siegel, Michael Strassfeld, Sharon Strassfeld
Jewish Publication Society
Philadelphia, Pennsylvania

God Was In This Place and I, i Did Not Know
Lawrence Kushner
Jewish Lights Publishing
Woodstock, Vermont

The Heavenly Ladder: The Jewish Guide to Inner Growth
Edward Hoffman
Harper and Row
San Francisco, California

Honey from the Rock
Lawrence Kushner
Jewish Lights Publishing
Woodstock, Vermont

The Lights of Penitence
Abraham Isaac Kook
trans. by Ben Zion Bokser
Paulist Press
Mahwah, New Jersey

Living Each Day
Abraham J. Twerski
Mesorah Publications
New York, New York

Nine Gates to the Chasidic Mysteries
Jiri Langer
Behrman House
West Orange, New Jersey

**One Hundred Blessings Every Day: Daily Twelve
Step Recovery Affirmations and Exercises for
Personal Growth and Renewal Reflecting Seasons
of the Jewish Year**
Kerry Olitzky
Jewish Lights Publishing
Woodstock, Vermont

Pirke Avot: Ethics for a New Age
Leonard Kravitz and Kerry Olitzky
Union of American Hebrew Congregations
New York, New York

**Recovery From Codependence: A Jewish Twelve
Steps Guide to Healing Your Soul**
Kerry Olitzky
Jewish Lights Publishing
Woodstock, Vermont

Renewed Each Day: Daily Twelve Step Recovery Meditations Based on the Bible in 2 Volumes
Kerry Olitzky and Aaron Z.
Jewish Lights Publishing
Woodstock, Vermont

The Sabbath
Abraham Joshua Heschel
Farrar, Straus, and Giroux
New York, New York

The Second Jewish Catalog
Michael and Sharon Strassfeld
Jewish Publication Society
Philadelphia, Pennsylvania

Self-Discovery in Recovery
Abraham J. Twerski
Hazelden Educational Materials
Center City, Minnesota

Teshuvah: A Guide for the Newly Observant Jew
Adin Steinsaltz trans. by Michael Swirsky
Free Press
New York, New York

The Third Jewish Catalog
Michael and Sharon Strassfeld
Jewish Publication Society
Philadelphia, Pennsylvania

The Twelve Steps and the Jewish Tradition
Susan Berman
Hazelden Educational Materials
Center City, Minnesota

Waking Up Just in Time
Abraham J. Twerski
Pharos Books
New York, New York

When do the Good Things Start?
Abraham J. Twerski
St. Martin's Press
New York, New York

About Us

Rabbi Kerry M. Olitzky, D.H.L., is National Dean of Adult Jewish Learning and Living at Hebrew Union College–Jewish Institute of Religion. At the forefront of Jewish education, he is the organizer of many programs on chemical dependency. Rabbi Olitzky is Special Issues Editor on Aging and Judaism for the *Journal of Psychology and Judaism*. He is Executive Editor of *Shofar* Magazine and is Chair of the Editorial Committee of *Compass* Magazine. He is the author of over 30 books and monographs and many articles on topics of Jewish interest.

Dr. Stuart A. Copans is Medical Director of The Adolescent Alcohol and Drug Treatment Program at the Brattleboro Retreat in Brattleboro, Vermont and Associate Professor of Clinical Psychiatry at Dartmouth Medical School in Hanover, New Hampshire. He is the author of many papers, abstracts, and other published works on the treatment of alcohol and drug abuse. Dr. Copans is also the talented illustrator of many books including the bestselling *The Jewish Catalog, The Second Jewish Catalog*, and *The Third Jewish Catalog*.

Dr. Abraham J. Twerski is a rabbi, psychiatrist, and an expert on recovery from addiction. He is medical director and founder of Gateway Rehabilitation Center in Aliquippa, Pennsylvania. Dr. Twerski is the author of many books on the subject of recovery including *Waking Up Just in Time, Self-Discovery in Recovery*, and *Living Each Day*.

Rabbi Sheldon Zimmerman was the Founder of the Task Force on Alcoholism of the Federation of Jewish Philanthropies of New York. When he was Rabbi of Central Synagogue in New York City, his congregation sponsored the first Alcoholics Anonymous group to meet in a synagogue. He is currently President of Hebrew Union College–Jewish Institute of Religion

Jeffrey Neipris and **David Buchholz** are Executive Director and President, respectively, of The JACS Foundation (Jewish Alcoholics, Chemically Dependent Persons and Significant Others) in New York City.

Maty Grünberg is an Israeli artist who has made his home in London since the late 1960s. His illuminated books and sculptures are found in the collections of museums and institutions throughout the world. In 1991 he completed a major limited edition print portfolio, *Jerusalem 1967-1990,* with poetry by Yehuda Amichai, published by the Friends of Bezalel Academy of Arts and Design, New York City.

About the Illustrations

Artist Maty Grünberg's illustrations of the gates of the Old City of Jerusalem open each chapter of the Twelve Steps as the reader is welcomed into another stage of a Jewish Twelve Steps experience. These were selected to emphasize the relationship between heavenly and earthly in all our lives through the prism of Jerusalem.

One enters a different plane of reality both physically and spiritually when entering the gates of the Old City. Our lives were changed by Jerusalem. Recognizing that at the center of the Jewish spiritual world is Jerusalem, we invited Maty Grünberg, to draw the gates of his beloved city so that you might enter it also, one gate at a time.

Motivation & Inspiration for Recovery

TWELVE JEWISH STEPS TO RECOVERY
A Personal Guide To Turning From Alcoholism & Other Addictions...Drugs, Food, Gambling, Sex

by *Rabbi Kerry M. Olitzky* & *Stuart A. Copans, M.D.*
Preface by Abraham J. Twerski, M.D.
Introduction by Rabbi Sheldon Zimmerman
Illustrations by Maty Grünberg
"Getting Help" by JACS Foundation

A Jewish perspective on the Twelve Steps of addiction recovery programs with consolation, inspiration and motivation for recovery. It draws from traditional sources, and quotes from what recovering Jewish people say about their experiences with addictions of all kinds. Inspiring illustrations of the twelve gates of the Old City of Jerusalem.

Experts Praise *Twelve Jewish Steps To Recovery*

Readers Praise *Twelve Jewish Steps To Recovery*

6" x 9", 136 pp. Quality Paperback, ISBN 1-879045-09-5 **$13.95**   HC, ISBN -08-7 **$19.95**

RECOVERY FROM *Codependence*
A Jewish Twelve Steps Guide to Healing Your Soul

by *Rabbi Kerry M. Olitzky*
Foreword by *Marc Galanter, M.D., Director, Division of Alcoholism & Drug Abuse, NYU Medical Center*
Afterword by *Harriet Rossetto, Director, Gateways Beit T'shuvah*

For the estimated 90% of America struggling with the addiction of a family member or loved one, or involved in a dysfunctional family or relationship. A follow-up to the groundbreaking *Twelve Jewish Steps to Recovery*.

6" x 9", 160 pp. Quality Paperback Original, ISBN 1-879045-32-X **$13.95**   HC, ISBN -27-3 **$21.95**

Motivation & Inspiration for Recovery

RENEWED EACH DAY
Daily Twelve Step Recovery Meditations
Based on the Bible
by *Rabbi Kerry M. Olitzky & Aaron Z.*

VOLUME I: Genesis & Exodus
Introduction by *Rabbi Michael A. Signer*
Afterword by JACS Foundation

VOLUME II: Leviticus, Numbers & Deuteronomy
Introduction by *Sharon M. Strassfeld*
Afterword by *Rabbi Harold M. Schulweis*

Using a seven day/weekly guide format, a recovering person and a spiritual leader who is reaching out to addicted people reflect on the traditional weekly Bible reading. They bring strong spiritual support for daily living and recovery from addictions of all kinds: alcohol, drugs, eating, gambling and sex. A profound sense of the religious spirit soars through their words and brings all people in Twelve Step recovery programs home to a rich and spiritually enlightening tradition.

"Meets a vital need; it offers a chance for people turning from alcoholism and addiction to renew their spirits and draw upon the Jewish tradition to guide and enrich their lives."
—*Rabbi Irving (Yitz) Greenberg, President, CLAL,*
The National Jewish Center for Learning and Leadership

"Will benefit anyone familiar with a 'religion of the Book.' Jews, Christians, Muslims. . . ."
—*Ernest Kurtz, author of* Not-God: A History of Alcoholics
Anonymous *&* The Spirituality of Imperfection

"An enduring impact upon the faith community as it seeks to blend the wisdom of the ages represented in the tradition with the twelve steps to recovery and wholeness."
—*Robert H. Albers, Ph.D., Editor,* Journal of Ministry in Addiction & Recovery

Beautiful Two-Volume Set.
6"x 9", V. I, 224 pp. / V. II, 280 pp., Quality Paperback, ISBN 1-879045-21-4   **$27.90**

---

100 BLESSINGS EVERY DAY
Daily Twelve Step Recovery
Affirmations & Exercises for
Personal Growth & Renewal
Reflecting Seasons of the Jewish Year
by *Dr. Kerry M. Olitzky*
with selected meditations prepared by *Rabbi James Stone Goodman, Danny Siegel,* and *Rabbi Gordon Tucker*
Foreword by *Rabbi Neil Gillman,*
The Jewish Theological Seminary of America
Afterword by *Dr. Jay Holder, Director, Exodus Treatment Center*

100 Blessings Every Day
Daily Twelve Step Recovery
Affirmations & Exercises for
Personal Growth & Renewal
Reflecting Seasons of the
Jewish Year
Kerry M.Olitzky
Foreword Are The Twelve Steps Jewish? by *Rabbi Neil Gillman*
Afterword Spiritual Renewal in the Jewish Calendar by *Sunday M. Holder*

Recovery is a conscious choice from moment to moment, day in and day out. In this helpful and healing book of daily recovery meditations, Kerry Olitzky gives us words to live by day after day, throughout the annual cycle of holiday obser-vances and special Sabbaths of the Jewish calendar.

For those facing the struggles of daily living, *One Hundred Blessings Every Day* brings solace and hope to anyone who is open to healing and to the recovery-oriented teach-ings that can be gleaned from the Bible and Jewish tradition.

4¹/2" x 6¹/2", Quality Paperback, 416 pp. ISBN 1-879045-30-3 **$14.95**
Available November 1993

12

Spirituality

GOD WAS IN THIS PLACE & I, i DID NOT KNOW
Finding Self, Spirituality & Ultimate Meaning
by Lawrence Kushner

Who am I? Who is God? Kushner creates inspiring interpretations of Jacob's dream in Genesis, opening a window into Jewish spirituality for people of all faiths and backgrounds.

In this fascinating blend of scholarship, imagination, psychology and history, seven Jewish spiritual masters ask and answer fundamental questions of human experience.

"Rich and intriguing."
—*M. Scott Peck, M.D., author of* The Road Less Traveled *and other books*

6" x 9", 192 pp. Quality Paperback, ISBN 1-879045-33-8 **$16.95** HC, ISBN -05-2 **$21.95**

THE RIVER OF LIGHT
Spirituality, Judaism, Consciousness
by Lawrence Kushner

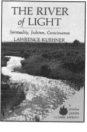

A "manual" for all spiritual travelers who would attempt a spiritual journey in our times. Taking us step by step, Kushner allows us to discover the meaning of our own quest: "to allow the river of light—the deepest currents of consciousness—to rise to the surface and animate our lives."

"Philosophy and mystical fantasy....Anybody—Jewish, Christian, or otherwise...will find this book an intriguing experience."
—*The Kirkus Reviews*

6" x 9", 180 pp. Quality Paperback, ISBN 1-879045-03-6 **$14.95**

SELF, STRUGGLE & CHANGE
Family Conflict Stories in Genesis
and Their Healing Insights for Our Lives
by *Norman J. Cohen*

How do I find greater wholeness in my life and in my family's life?
The stress of late-20th-century living only brings new variations to timeless personal struggles. The people described in Genesis were in situations and relationships very much like our own. Their stories still speak to us because they are about the same problems we deal with every day. A modern master of biblical interpretation brings us greater understanding of the ancient text and of ourselves in this intriguing re-telling of conflict between husband and wife, father and son, brothers, and sisters.

"A delightful and instructive book; recommended."
—*Library Journal*
6" x 9", 224 pp. Quality Paperback, ISBN 1-879045-66-4 **$16.95**   HC, ISBN -19-2 **$21.95**

BEING GOD'S PARTNER
How to Find the Hidden Link Between
Spirituality and Your Work
by *Jeffrey K. Salkin* Introduction by *Norman Lear*

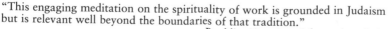

A book that will challenge people of every denomination to reconcile the cares of work and soul. A groundbreaking book about spirituality and the work world, from a Jewish perspective. Helps the reader find God in the ethical striving and search for meaning in the professions and in business and offers practical suggestions for balancing your professional life and spiritual self.

"This engaging meditation on the spirituality of work is grounded in Judaism but is relevant well beyond the boundaries of that tradition."
—Booklist *(American Library Association)*

6" x 9", 192 pp. Quality Paperback, ISBN 1-879045-65-6 **$16.95** HC, ISBN -37-0 **$19.95**

Spirituality

HOW TO BE A PERFECT STRANGER, In 2 Volumes
A Guide to Etiquette in Other People's
Religious Ceremonies
Edited by Stuart M. Matlins & Arthur J. Magida

"A book that belongs in every living room, library and office!"

Explains the rituals and celebrations of America's major religions/denominations, helping an interested guest to feel comfortable, participate to the fullest extent possible, and avoid violating anyone's religious principles. Answers practical questions from the perspective of *any* other faith.

VOL. 1: America's Largest Faiths

VOL. 1 COVERS: Assemblies of God • Baptist • Buddhist • Christian Science • Churches of Christ • Disciples of Christ • Episcopalian • Greek Orthodox • Hindu • Islam • Jehovah's Witnesses • Jewish • Lutheran • Methodist • Mormon • Presbyterian • Quaker • Roman Catholic • Seventh-day Adventist • United Church of Christ

6" x 9", 432 pp. Hardcover, ISBN 1-879045-39-7 **$24.95**

VOL. 2: Other Faiths in America

VOL. 2 COVERS: African American Methodist Churches • Baha'i • Christian and Missionary Alliance • Christian Congregation • Church of the Brethren • Church of the Nazarene • Evangelical Free Church of America • International Church of the Foursquare Gospel • International Pentecostal Holiness Church • Mennonite/Amish • Native American • Orthodox Churches • Pentecostal Church of God • Reformed Church of America • Sikh • Unitarian Universalist • Wesleyan

6" x 9", 416 pp. Hardcover, ISBN 1-879045-63-X **$24.95**

GOD & THE BIG BANG
Discovering Harmony Between Science & Spirituality
by *Daniel C. Matt*

Mysticism and science: What do they have in common? How can one enlighten the other? By drawing on modern cosmology and ancient Kabbalah, Matt shows how science and religion can together enrich our spiritual awareness and help us recover a sense of wonder and find our place in the universe.

"This poetic new book...helps us to understand the human meaning of creation."
—*Joel Primack, leading cosmologist, Professor of Physics, University of California, Santa Cruz*

6" x 9", 216 pp. Hardcover, ISBN 1-879045-48-6 **$21.95**

MINDING THE TEMPLE OF THE SOUL
Balancing Body, Mind & Spirit through Traditional Jewish Prayer, Movement & Meditation
by *Tamar Frankiel* and *Judy Greenfeld*

This new spiritual approach to physical health introduces readers to a spiritual tradition that affirms the body. Relying on Kabbalistic teachings and other Jewish traditions, it focuses on the discipline of prayer, simple exercises and body positions, and guides the reader throughout, step by step.

7" x 10", 184 pp, Quality Paperback Original, illus., ISBN 1-879045-64-8 $15.95

Audiotape of the Prayers, Movements & Meditations (60-min. cassette) **$9.95**

SPIRITUALITY...Other books

Healing of Soul, Healing of Body: Spiritual Leaders Unfold the Strength and Solace in Psalms

Ed. by Rabbi Simkha Y. Weintraub, CSW, for The Jewish Healing Center

6" x 9", 128 pp, Quality Paperback Original, illus., 2-color text, ISBN 1-879045-31-1 **$14.95**

Life Cycle

A HEART OF WISDOM
Making the Jewish Journey from Midlife Through the Aging Years
Edited by *Susan Berrin*

We are all growing older. *A Heart of Wisdom* shows us how to understand our own process of aging—and the aging of those we care about—from a Jewish perspective, from midlife through the elder years.

How does Jewish tradition influence our own aging? How does living, thinking and worshipping as a Jew affect us as we age? How can Jewish tradition help us retain our dignity as we age? Offers insights and enlightenment from Jewish tradition.

"A must for all ages at all stages."
—*Ruth Perelson, Chair Emerita, Jewish Assoc. for Services for the Aged of Greater New York*

6" x 9", 304 pp. (est.) HC, ISBN 1-879045-73-7 **$24.95**

EMBRACING THE COVENANT
Converts to Judaism Talk About Why & How
Edited & with Intros. by *Rabbi Allan L. Berkowitz* and *Patti Moskovitz*

A practical and inspirational companion to the conversion process for Jews-by-Choice and their families. It provides highly personal insights from over 50 people who have made this life-changing decision.

"Passionate, thoughtful and deeply felt personal stories....A wonderful resource, sure to light the way for many who choose to follow the same path."
—*Dru Greenwood, MSW, Director, UAHC-CCAR Commission on Reform Jewish Outreach*

6" x 9", 192 pp. Quality Paperback, ISBN 1-879045-50-8 **$15.95**

LIFECYCLES
V. 1: Jewish Women on Life Passages & Personal Milestones
Edited and with introductions by *Rabbi Debra Orenstein*
V. 2: Jewish Women on Biblical Themes in Contemporary Life
Edited and with introductions by
Rabbi Debra Orenstein and *Rabbi Jane Rachel Litman*

This unique three-volume collaboration brings together over one hundred women writers, rabbis, and scholars to create the first comprehensive work on Jewish life cycle that fully includes women's perspectives.

"Nothing is missing from this marvelous collection. You will turn to it for rituals and inspiration, prayer and poetry, comfort and community. *Lifecycles* is a gift to the Jewish woman in America."
—*Letty Cottin Pogrebin, author of* Deborah, Golda, and Me: Being Female and Jewish in America

V. 1: 6 x 9, 480 pp. HC, ISBN 1-879045-14-1, **$24.95**; **V. 2:** 6 x 9, 464 pp. HC, ISBN 1-879045-15-X, **$24.95**

LIFE CYCLE...Other books— The Art of Jewish Living Series for Holiday Observance
by Dr. Ron Wolfson

Hanukkah—7" x 9", 192 pp. Quality Paperback, ISBN 1-879045-97-4 **$16.95**

The Shabbat Seder—7" x 9", 272 pp, Quality Paperback, ISBN 1-879045-90-7 **$16.95**; Booklet of Blessings **$5.00**; Audiocassette of Blessings **$6.00**; Teacher's Guide **$4.95**

The Passover Seder—7" x 9", 272 pp, Quality Paperback, ISBN 1-879045-90-7 **$16.95**; Passover Workbook, **$6.95**; Audiocassette of Blessings, **$6.00**; Teacher's Guide, **$4.95**

Life Cycle

MOURNING & MITZVAH
• With over 60 guided exercises •
A Guided Journal for Walking the Mourner's Path Through Grief to Healing
by *Anne Brener, L.C.S.W.*; Foreword by *Rabbi Jack Riemer*; Introduction by *Rabbi William Cutter*

"Fully engaging in mourning means you will be a different person than before you began." For those who mourn a death, for those who would help them, for those who face a loss of any kind, Brener teaches us the power and strength available to us in the fully experienced mourning process. Guided writing exercises help stimulate the processes of both conscious and unconscious healing.

"A stunning book! It offers an exploration in depth of the place where psychology and religious ritual intersect, and the name of that place is Truth."
—*Rabbi Harold Kushner, author of* When Bad Things Happen to Good People

7 1/2" x 9", 288 pp. Quality Paperback Original, ISBN 1-879045-23-0 **$19.95**

A TIME TO MOURN, A TIME TO COMFORT
A Guide to Jewish Bereavement and Comfort
by *Dr. Ron Wolfson*

A guide to meeting the needs of those who mourn and those who seek to provide comfort in times of sadness. While this book is written from a layperson's point of view, it also includes the specifics for funeral preparations and practical guidance for preparing the home and family to sit *shiva*.

"A sensitive and perceptive guide to Jewish tradition. Both those who mourn and those who comfort will find it a map to accompany them through the whirlwind."
—*Deborah E. Lipstadt, Emory University*

7" x 9", 320 pp. Quality Paperback, ISBN 1-879045-96-6 **$16.95**

WHEN A GRANDPARENT DIES
A Kid's Own Remembering Workbook for Dealing with Shiva and the Year Beyond
by *Nechama Liss-Levinson, Ph.D.*

Drawing insights from both psychology and Jewish tradition, this workbook helps children participate in the process of mourning, offering guided exercises, rituals, and places to write, draw, list, create and express their feelings.

"Will bring support, guidance, and understanding for countless children, teachers, and health professionals."
—*Rabbi Earl A. Grollman, D.D., author of* Talking about Death

8" x 10", 48 pp. Hardcover, illus., 2-color text, ISBN 1-879045-44-3 **$14.95**

LIFE CYCLE...Other books

Bar/Bat Mitzvah Basics: A Practical Family Guide to Coming of Age Together
Ed. by Cantor Helen Leneman

6" x 9", 240 pp, Quality Paperback, ISBN 1-879045-54-0 **$16.95**; HC, ISBN -51-6 **$24.95**

The New Jewish Baby Book: Names, Ceremonies, Customs—A Guide for Today's Families by Anita Diamant

6" x 9", 328 pp, Quality Paperback, ISBN 1-879045-28-1 **$16.95**

Putting God on the Guest List, 2nd Ed.: How to Reclaim the Spiritual Meaning of Your Child's Bar or Bat Mitzvah
by Rabbi Jeffrey K. Salkin

6" x 9", 224 pp, Quality Paperback, ISBN 1-897045-59-1 **$16.95**; HC, ISBN -58-3 **$24.95**

So That Your Values Live On: Ethical Wills & How to Prepare Them
Ed. by Rabbi Jack Riemer & Professor Nathaniel Stampfer

6" x 9", 272 pp, Quality Paperback, ISBN 1-879045-34-6 **$17.95**

Theology/Philosophy

ISRAEL
An Echo of Eternity
by *Abraham Joshua Heschel* with New Introduction by *Susannah Heschel*

In this classic reprint originally published by Farrar, Straus & Giroux, one of the foremost religious figures of our century gives us a powerful and eloquent statement on the meaning of Israel in our time. Heschel looks at the past, present and future home of the Jewish people. He tells us how and why the presence of Israel has tremendous historical and religious significance for the whole world.

5 1/2" x 8", 272 pp. Quality Paperback Original, ISBN 1-879045-70-2 **$18.95**

THE SPIRIT OF RENEWAL
Finding Faith After the Holocaust
by *Edward Feld*

"Boldly redefines the landscape of Jewish religious thought after the Holocaust."
—*Rabbi Lawrence Kushner*

Trying to understand the Holocaust and addressing the question of faith after the Holocaust, Rabbi Feld explores three key cycles of destruction and recovery in Jewish history, each of which radically reshaped Jewish understanding of God, people, and the world.

"A profound meditation on Jewish history [and the Holocaust]....Christians, as well as many others, need to share in this story."
—*The Rt. Rev. Frederick H. Borsch, Ph.D., Episcopal Bishop of L.A.*

• AWARD WINNER •

6" x 9", 224 pp. Quality Paperback, ISBN 1-879045-40-0 **$16.95**   HC, ISBN-06-0 **$22.95**

SEEKING THE PATH TO LIFE
Theological Meditations On God
and the Nature of People, Love, Life and Death
by *Rabbi Ira F. Stone*

For people who never thought they would read a book of theology—let alone understand it, enjoy it, savor it and have it affect the way they think about their lives. In 45 intense meditations, each a page or two in length, Stone takes us on explorations of the most basic human struggles: Life and death, love and anger, peace and war, covenant and exile.

• AWARD WINNER •   "A bold book....The reader of any faith will be inspired...."
— *The Rev. Carla V. Berkedal, Episcopal Priest*

6" x 9", 132 pp. Quality Paperback, ISBN 1-879045-47-8 **$14.95**   HC, ISBN-17-6 **$19.95**

THEOLOGY & PHILOSOPHY...Other books—Classic Reprints

Tormented Master: The Life and Spiritual Quest of Rabbi Nahman of Bratslav
by Arthur Green
6" x 9", 408 pp, Quality Paperback, ISBN 1-879045-11-7 **$18.95**

The Earth Is the Lord's: The Inner World of the Jew in Eastern Europe
by Abraham Joshua Heschel with woodcut illustrations by Ilya Schor
5 1/2" x 8", 112 pp, Quality Paperback, ISBN 1-879045-42-7 **$13.95**

A Passion for Truth by Abraham Joshua Heschel
5 1/2" x 8", 352 pp, Quality Paperback, ISBN 1-879045-41-9 **$18.95**

Your Word Is Fire
Edited and translated with a new introduction by Arthur Green and Barry W. Holtz
6" x 9", 152 pp, Quality Paperback, ISBN 1-879045-25-7 **$14.95**

Aspects of Rabbinic Theology
by Solomon Schechter, with a New Introduction by Neil Gillman
6" x 9", 440 pp, Quality Paperback, ISBN 1-879045-24-9 **$18.95**

The Last Trial: On the Legends and Lore of the Command to Abraham to Offer Isaac as a Sacrifice by Shalom Spiegel, with a new introduction by Judah Goldin
6" x 9", 208 pp, Quality Paperback, ISBN 1-879045-29-X **$17.95**

Children's Spirituality

For ages 8 and up

BUT GOD REMEMBERED
Stories of Women from Creation to the Promised Land
by *Sandy Eisenberg Sasso*
Full color illustrations by *Bethanne Andersen*

NONSECTARIAN, NONDENOMINATIONAL.

A fascinating collection of four different stories of women only briefly mentioned in biblical tradition and religious texts, but never before explored. Award-winning author Sasso brings to life the intriguing stories of Lilith, Serach, Bityah, and the Daughters of Z, courageous and strong women from ancient tradition. All teach important values through their faith and actions.

•AWARD WINNER•

"Exquisite....a book of beauty, strength and spirituality."
—*Association of Bible Teachers*

9" x 12", 32 pp. Hardcover, Full color illus., ISBN 1-879045-43-5 **$16.95**

IN GOD'S NAME
by *Sandy Eisenberg Sasso*
Full color illustrations by *Phoebe Stone*

For ages 4-8

MULTICULTURAL, NONSECTARIAN, NONDENOMINATIONAL.

Like an ancient myth in its poetic text and vibrant illustrations, this modern fable about the search for God's name celebrates the diversity and, at the same time, the unity of all the people of the world. Each seeker claims he or she alone knows the answer. Finally, they come together and learn what God's name really is, sharing the ultimate harmony of belief in one God by people of all faiths, all backgrounds.

•AWARD WINNER•   "I got goose bumps when I read *In God's Name*, its language and illustrations are that moving. This is a book children will love and the whole family will cherish for its beauty and power."
—*Francine Klagsbrun, author of* Mixed Feelings: Love, Hate, Rivalry, and Reconciliation among Brothers and Sisters

"What a lovely, healing book!"
—*Madeleine L'Engle*

> Selected by
> Parent Council Ltd.™

9" x 12", 32 pp. Hardcover, Full color illus., ISBN 1-879045-26-5 **$16.95**

For ages 4-8

GOD'S PAINTBRUSH
by *Sandy Eisenberg Sasso*
Full color illustrations by *Annette Compton*

MULTICULTURAL, NONSECTARIAN, NONDENOMINATIONAL.

Invites children of all faiths and backgrounds to encounter God openly in their own lives. Wonderfully interactive, provides questions adult and child can explore together at the end of each episode.

"An excellent way to honor the imaginative breadth and depth of the spiritual life of the young."
—*Dr. Robert Coles, Harvard University*

•AWARD WINNER•

11" x 8 1/2", 32 pp. Hardcover, Full color illus., ISBN 1-879045-22-2 **$16.95**

Also Available!
Teacher's Guide: A Guide for Jewish & Christian Educators and Parents
8 1/2" x 11", 32 pp. Paperback, ISBN 1-879045-57-5 **$6.95**

Children's Spirituality
ENDORSED BY CATHOLIC, PROTESTANT AND JEWISH RELIGIOUS LEADERS

A PRAYER FOR THE EARTH
The Story of Naamah, Noah's Wife

For ages 4-8

by *Sandy Eisenberg Sasso*
Full color illustrations by *Bethanne Andersen*

NONSECTARIAN, NONDENOMINATIONAL.

This new story, based on an ancient text, opens readers' religious imaginations to new ideas about the well-known story of the Flood. When God tells Noah to bring the animals of the world onto the ark, God *also* calls on Naamah, Noah's wife, to save each plant on Earth. *A Prayer for the Earth* describes Naamah's wisdom and love for the natural harmony of the earth, and inspires readers to use their own courage, creativity and faith to carry out Naamah's work today.

•AWARD WINNER•

"A lovely tale....Children of all ages should be drawn to this parable for our times."
—*Tomie dePaola, artist/author of books for children*

9" x 12", 32 pp. Hardcover, Full color illus., ISBN 1-879045-60-5 **$16.95**

THE 11TH COMMANDMENT
Wisdom from Our Children
For all ages

by The Children of America

MULTICULTURAL, NONSECTARIAN, NONDENOMINATIONAL.

"If there were an Eleventh Commandment, what would it be?"

Children of many religious denominations across America answer this question—in their own drawings and words—in *The 11th Commandment*. This full-color collection of "Eleventh Commandments" reveals kids' ideas about how people should respond to God.

"Wonderful....This unusual book provides both food for thought and insight into the hopes and fears of today's young."
—*American Library Association's* Booklist

8" x 10", 48 pp. Hardcover, Full color illus., ISBN 1-879045-46-X **$16.95**

SHARING BLESSINGS
Children's Stories for Exploring the Spirit of the Jewish Holidays

For ages 6-10

by *Rahel Musleah* and *Rabbi Michael Klayman*
Full color illustrations by *Mary O'Keefe Young*

**What is the spiritual message of each of the Jewish holidays?
How do we teach it to our children?**

Many books tell children about the historical significance and customs of the holidays. Now, through engaging, creative stories about one family's spiritual preparation, *Sharing Blessings* explores ways to get into the *spirit* of the holidays all year long. For 13 different holidays and festivals, there is a story about David, Ilana, and their mom and dad—a story focusing on the spiritual value embodied in each holiday. Each story concludes with a special prayer that child and adult can share to bring the spiritual meaning of the holiday into their own lives.

"A beguiling introduction to important Jewish values by way of the holidays."
—*Rabbi Harold Kushner, author of* When Bad Things Happen to Good People *and* How Good Do We Have to Be?

7" x 10", 64 pp. Hardcover, Full color illus., ISBN 1-879045-71-0 **$18.95**

Order Information

# of Copies	Book Title / ISBN (Last 3 digits)	$ Amount
_____	_____	_____
_____	_____	_____
_____	_____	_____
_____	_____	_____
_____	_____	_____
_____	_____	_____
_____	_____	_____
_____	_____	_____
_____	_____	_____
_____	_____	_____
_____	_____	_____
_____	_____	_____
_____	_____	_____

For s/h, add $3.50 for the first book, $2.00 each add'l book
(to a max of $15.00) $ S/H _____

TOTAL _____

Check enclosed for $_____ *payable to:* JEWISH LIGHTS Publishing

Charge my credit card: ❑ MasterCard ❑ Visa

Credit Card #_____Expires _____

Signature _____Phone (_____)_____

Your Name _____

Street_____

City / State / Zip _____

Ship To:

Name _____

Street_____

City / State / Zip _____

Phone, fax or mail to: **JEWISH LIGHTS Publishing**
P.O. Box 237 • Sunset Farm Offices, Route 4 • Woodstock, Vermont 05091
Tel (802) 457-4000   Fax (802) 457-4004   www.jewishlights.com
Credit card orders **(800) 962-4544** (9AM–5PM ET Monday–Friday)
Generous discounts on quantity orders. SATISFACTION GUARANTEED. Prices subject to change.